HOW TO HAVE AN ADVENTURE IN
SCANDINAVIA
-NORWAY & DENMARK-
RAFFAEL CORONELLI

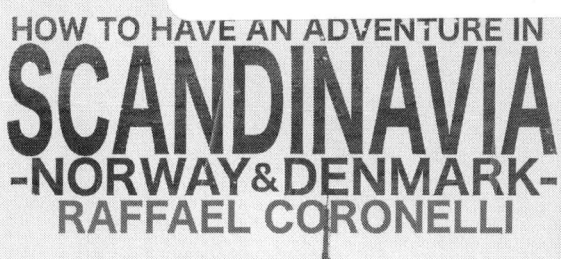

By Raffael Coronelli

Nonfiction

HOW TO HAVE AN ADVENTURE IN NORTHERN JAPAN

HOW TO HAVE AN ADVENTURE IN SCOTLAND

HOW TO HAVE AN ADVENTURE IN SCANDINAVIA: NORWAY & DENMARK

HOW TO HAVE AN ADVENTURE IN TRANSYLVANIA

Novels

DAIKAIJU YUKI

Y2K: YUKI CONQUERS THE WORLD

YUKI VS. FLESHWORLD

MOKWA: LIFESBLOOD OF THE EARTH

MOKWA: URSA MAJOR

MOKWA: EXORCISM

BIG EGG

Novellas

SCYTHIAN FROST AND OTHER STORIES

PHARAOH OF EELS

Praise for Raffael Coronelli's travel books

"Raffael continues to have a mastery of adventure... few people capture a sense of place better."
-Andrew Roebuck, *Scriptophobic.ca*

"Raffael Coronelli doesn't just make you want to travel... He makes you feel as though you've already visited."
-Marie Matsui, *Marie's Yokai Adventures*

"Each locale is more than a series of events, it's a personality and Coronelli unveils it to us through intimate interactions with the people and places therein."
-Alex Gayhart, author of *All Your Ruins*

"Coronelli takes readers on a whimsical journey... Both descriptively complex and invigoratingly giddy."
-Donny Winter, author of *Carbon Footprint*

"Raffael's book lets our feet wander and minds wonder along with him."
-Lisa Naffziger, creator of *Taking Back Tokusatsu*

How to Have an Adventure in Scandinavia: Norway & Denmark

Copyright © 2022 Raffael Coronelli

Photography by Raffael Coronelli

Original illustration by Alex Gayhart

All rights reserved. No part of this book may be reproduced in any manner whatsoever without written permission, except in the case of brief quotations embodied in critical or analytical articles, reviews, or discussions.

Views and opinions expressed in this book are solely those of the author and do not reflect those of persons or organizations mentioned or depicted.

LEGO® is a trademark of LEGO Group, who do not approve or endorse this book.

This book is based on true events, unless otherwise stated in the text. Fiction segments, as denoted by the author, are products of the author's imagination.

Content warning:
This book contains references to violent events that some may consider upsetting.

ISBN: 9798845988652

First Edition: October 2022

Hails and dedications
to everyone I've met in Scandinavia.

Thanks and acknowledgements
for artistic and/or informative input from
Kristian "Gaahl" Espedal,
Robin Jacobsen, Kim Diaz Holm,
Tonje Sommerli, Vlada Niskova,
Professor Laura Saetveit Miles at the University of Bergen,
Senior Advisor to the U.S. State Department's
Coordinator for the Arctic Region Hillary LeBail,
and the illustration talents of Alex Gayhart.

The Sognefjord, Norway

RAFFAEL CORONELLI
PRESENTS

Icy winds howl across churning seas between sheer mountainsides. A never-setting sun reflects off snowcapped peaks. Ornate castles loom over waters traversed by longships of bygone eras.

Imagery like this drew me to Scandinavia. Amidst my adventures across the world, these countries at the top of Europe promised a specific flavor that had always fascinated me and made me want to someday go.

When it came time to plan my first international trip in two and a half years, my first time overseas since the start of the pandemic, I jumped at the opportunity. Being able to go abroad again had a certain symbolic quality. I had to make my first trip a good one, something that satisfied long-term interests and gave back a sense of vitality and adventure.

Norway and Denmark had everything I'd desired and more.

HOW TO HAVE AN ADVENTURE IN SCANDINAVIA

Arrival in Oslo:
Labyrinths and Øl

I think I got close to Valhalla somewhere over the Atlantic. Long haul flights are the last thing a sane person would think they'd miss. That was before the pandemic, before the annihilation of fun international travel for years. After being trapped by a plague that shook the foundations of civilization, we'd pulled through. There will always be some darkness. To live is to continue through it.

Vaccination record card in my passport holder, I'd miraculously gotten a whole row to myself in a Lufthansa airliner's coach class where I could lay back, unplugged from the internet and washing down a German beer as I drifted in and out of sleep. Somehow, this was euphoria.

It was the third of May, 2022, and this was my first entry to another country in nearly two and a half years — the last time being my adventure through northern Japan in December 2019. Everything had lead to this moment.

With a few hours to kill at my lunchtime layover in the Munich airport, I grabbed a leberkase (a traditional Germanic liver sausage) sandwich and a mug of delicious Hofbräuhaus lager, a must in the Bavarian city for those who partake in such beverages. A small taste of Germany before heading north, it was just enough to tide me over — and the perfect setup.

RAFFAEL CORONELLI

The story of the Scandinavian region's human cultures and a familiar helmet shape begins well before recorded history in the murky depths of pre-Roman Central Europe, when Germanic tribes wandered northward. An artifact in Copenhagen's National Museum of Denmark dated vaguely to the mid-to-late Bronze Age (anywhere between 1400 and 800 BC) depicts a chariot pulling the Sun — a depiction that appears in a number of ancient civilizations through convergent cultural evolution.

Conical and amusingly tall golden hats that could've been worn by Bronze Age priests to the Sun have also been found in Germany, painting a picture of an exotic prehistoric culture and belief system.

Experts like those at the National Museum of Denmark believe the extravagant hat-wearing Germanic Sun Cult could've been a precursor to the Norse culture that would follow when such tribes ventured beyond the extent of the Roman Empire's coming expansion and into a peninsula north of Germany known as Jutland (linguistically tied to the English verb to "jut" out of something), now a large section of modern Denmark.

This Bronze Age pre-Viking civilization in Denmark were the ones responsible for the horned helmets often attributed to the cartoon Viking image. While their fabulous hats would go out of fashion, they would lay the foundations for Nordic culture in Scandinavia — a culture that would spread through the Vikings' global influence.

They were not, however, the only ones to populate the region in early periods. The Sami, originators of what would become Finnish culture and language, are the indigenous people to the arctic regions of Norway, Sweden, and Finland. Not tied to Germanic roots, they migrated from the east through Finland, their language part of the Uralic family of Eastern Europe. This unique people still lives in and influences Scandinavia's Arctic across national boundaries, including northern Norway.

HOW TO HAVE AN ADVENTURE IN SCANDINAVIA

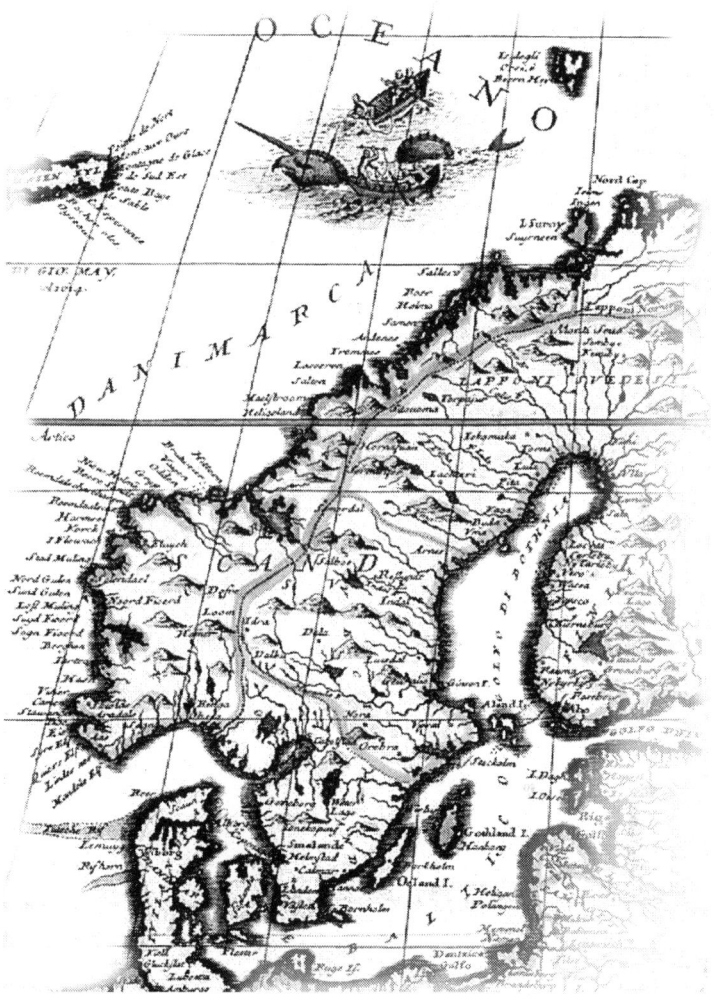

The Scandinavian region,
excerpt from a map by Vincenzo Coronelli, c 1690

This gives us a good basis for what/where exactly "Scandinavia" is, and how it relates to the "Nordic" countries. Scandinavia refers to the area around the Scandinavian Peninsula that includes Norway and Sweden, with Denmark situated just below it. By geographic and historical proximity, Finland can also be considered Scandinavian, though it has its own rich cultural history tying back to the Sami, as well as some Russian imperial influence from the east.

The Nordic countries, on the other hand, are a broader sphere shaped by Viking cultural migration that also includes mid-Atlantic Iceland and, to an extent, North American Greenland (a territory of Denmark today). The two countries featured in this book are both predominantly Nordic in cultural background and Scandinavian in geography. Sweden is the only other country that shares this distinction.

Speaking of Sweden, it was simply too big for this trip. Traversing it and taking in its sights would take up more time and finances than I'd allotted, and would need another trip to appreciate. Instead, I turned my full attention to the westernmost Scandinavian nations, Norway and Denmark. This allowed me to map out a two-and-a-half-week, north-south excursion that would straddle Scandinavia's latitudes, vistas, flavors, and the progression of its rich history.

My saga would begin in Oslo. Then I'd go west to Bergen, then up by boat into the Sognefjord. Then I'd fly into the high reaches of arctic Tromsø, beyond the limits of day and night. After Norway, I'd travel south by sea to Copenhagen, crown of Denmark that allows access to the sprawling sights on the island of Zealand. I'd end my trip by crossing into Jutland, where Denmark juts northward from Germany.

HOW TO HAVE AN ADVENTURE IN SCANDINAVIA

Out of Germany was indeed my trajectory. In no time, I was seated on the slightly smaller Airbus headed due north. The Kattegat passed below, Sweden to the east as we flew over the chilled straight I'd later traverse by sea voyage, which the Vikings sailed countless times between their realms. At the end of it opened the yawning mouth of Norway drinking in the waves — the Oslofjord, a beckoning gateway beyond which lay an adventure through unconquerable landscapes, monstrous legends, and a legacy of northern darkness.

NORWAY

RAFFAEL CORONELLI

The Oslofjord

My first impressions of Norway out the plane window were its rugged landscape. The southern parts of the country are further north than the Scottish highlands, and look the part. The furthest from the equator I'd been before had been Uig on Scotland's Isle of Skye, with a latitude of 57.58° N. In comparison, Oslo in Southern Norway is 59.9° N, and suitably heightened in its topography. Tall, narrow Norway Spruce trees dotted hillsides in toothpick-like groves.

Soon, I was on the ground and through baggage claim. Going through border control is unnecessary if you've already done it in Europe's Schengen Zone, a group of countries that share open borders with each other. All Scandinavian countries are in the Schengen Zone, so a trip to the region can cross borders at will. I'd cleared customs in Germany and could freely enter Norway without hassle.

A short ride on the airport express later, I was in Oslo Sentralstasjon. Emerging from the platform into the main hall of the station, its utilitarian design prepped me for one of central Oslo's main aesthetics — modern brutalist architecture with a grey-brown color scheme. It's not a beautiful building, but it is well planned out and easy to navigate, one of the most convenient and comprehensible large train stations I've used. Don't let it fool you into thinking the rest of Oslo will be the same.

HOW TO HAVE AN ADVENTURE IN SCANDINAVIA

On a list ranking major cities of the world by how close their street system is to a grid layout, Oslo is near last. This is a medieval city built around winding streets that twist through hills and fjordside crevices, with modern roads built on old paths that sometimes cross over each other on different levels. No two sides of a block will lead you to the same place.

This realization not yet fully set in, it was then I realized that my phone's 5G would not be working well in Norway. Luckily, I was able to connect to free nearby wi-fi (common in Norway) and screenshot a map and directions to follow the old fashioned, harder way — without GPS.

The path from the train station into the Youngstorget neighborhood where my hotel was located was a brutalist concrete labyrinth, a grim and grimy maze under perpetual construction at every turn — turns which inevitably had to be backtracked since I kept getting lost.

Blue trams rumbled by on tracks in the middle of the street. I like seeing different methods of public transit in different parts of the world, and Oslo's tram system is a good way to get around the city. You can buy a ticket at kiosks which take some time to find, like anything in Oslo — or, you can find an internet connection and download an app to buy a digital pass. More on my experience riding these things later.

Unfortunately, the trams only go so many places, and I had to continue my trek to Youngstorget on foot. I'd get better at this walk as my stay progressed, but I'd just gotten off the plane. Full luggage in hand, I descended further into central Oslo's grimy labyrinth.

You might think, in the current year, why couldn't I just call up an Uber? That's because ride sharing and especially Uber have a dubious legality in Norway due to the company's interference with heavily enforced union laws and licenses.

In Denmark, Uber is outright illegal and the company has no operations there. In Norway, drivers with approved taxi licenses can drive more expensive Uber Black and XL ride shares if you don't mind paying for them, but both are steeper in price than the standard Oslo taxi. If you absolutely can't navigate the streets of Oslo, your best bet for the price would be a regular taxi.

Despite my griping, I never had to use a taxi service in the city, thereby saving a lot of money, getting a lot of exercise, and strengthening my brain with the mind puzzles of following the lucid disarray of Oslo's streets.

A helpful element proved to be landmarks. I passed Oslo Street Food, a food hall popular with young people filled with international cuisine options. Oslo has a young, fashionable populace who always seem to be in a hurry when walking anywhere. Mathallen (literally "the food hall"), which I did not get to try, is another one a little bit north of the area in which I stayed, and has a number of slightly higher end options. It inconveniently closes at 5:00 PM, but eateries in Oslo sometimes have strange hours.

I mentioned the harsh, grimy aesthetic of this part of Oslo, but I never once felt unsafe. Oslo is an incredibly safe city, where people from all backgrounds live. Countless city workers moved around the streets, constantly busy.

Oslo has a wide array of immigrants, many from the Middle East with some Africans and East Asians. Norwegians of Middle Eastern descent have contributed the country's most widespread fast food option, the kabob shop. From what I saw in Norway, a fast food place not part of an American chain almost always had döner alongside the usual hamburgers and whatnot.

One might be lead to believe that this is exclusively a recent development, but history suggests otherwise. The Vikings visited areas as far as North Africa, engaging in cultural exchange and bringing things back. International influence is going strong in 21st Century Oslo.

HOW TO HAVE AN ADVENTURE IN SCANDINAVIA

Plenty of typically Viking-looking guys and tall blonde ladies hurried along Oslo's sidewalks. Norwegians are direct, and people don't quite mosey around.

My hotel in Youngstorget wasn't much to write about, a standard business hotel with a single occupancy room. I often say in these situations, "you get what you pay for, and you didn't pay for much." In hindsight, I would've preferred a hotel with at least breakfast included considering my ordeal the following morning, but its location was perfect for what I wanted to do that evening.

The Youngstorget neighborhood is notable for one thing in particular — bars. You'll always find some place to have a drink in this bustling area. I knew of one in particular I wanted to try, located on the same block as my hotel, a gift from the gods to ease my navigation challenges. Checked in with my things dropped into the hotel room, I headed down the block for my first sampling of contemporary Norwegian culture at a bar called Kniven — literally "the knife."

I'd heard about Kniven in my research before coming to the city, its reputation riding on three things. Two are other businesses to which it shares close proximity and connections — the music venue Revolver, and one of Oslo's best regarded craft microbreweries, Beer Flag. The third draw of which I'd heard is that this bar's vibe taps into the darker side of Norwegian pop culture. Not everyone reading this will want to dive into the deep end on arrival and may prefer to opt for one of the other establishments in Youngstorget. Personally, I was ready.

It was about 8:00 PM as I headed down the street to the bar — broad daylight in Oslo in May. Southern Norway doesn't get the midnight sun like the arctic region does, but daylight does stick around longer than anywhere to the south. The light level changed as I pulled the door open to the entry hall lined with show posters for bands playing at the nearby Revolver club.

RAFFAEL CORONELLI

Interior decor in Kniven

HOW TO HAVE AN ADVENTURE IN SCANDINAVIA

Dark artwork and strange taxidermy props lined the walls. The cooky decor set a tone matched by Black Metal playing at a reasonable volume — a playlist curated in real time by the bar tender. Seating myself next to a demonic taxidermy goat, I motioned to get the bar tender's attention.

"Jeg vil ha," Norwegian for 'I will have,' I started in what was probably a ridiculous American accent.

He laughed and handed me a beer menu.

"Here you go," he said in English, a little skittish and nervous at his English abilities but much better than my attempt at Norwegian.

There's no language barrier in Oslo. Further north, I'd encounter a few older people who spoke less English, but everyone in Oslo and under a certain age is completely fluent.

"What Beer Flag beers do you recommend?" I asked. "It's made right over there, right?"

I pointed out the window to the brewery next door.

"Yes!" he said excitedly, possibly surprised that I knew about the microbrewery.

Still a little nervous, he showed some reluctance to give me one single recommendation from Beer Flag's arsenal, instead giving me a run through of every one of their offerings. I chose their "Killer Kølsj" (a lighter German kölsch style). Smooth and lager-adjacent, it was perfect for whetting the appetite for more Norwegian øl (beer, in a word that is clearly related to the English term "ale").

He handed me the portable card reader so I could pay. Bar tabs aren't really a thing in Norway, and you pay for each drink one at a time. It might take you aback at first, like you're being kicked out after one drink, but this is just the way it's done and they're perfectly happy to serve you more on your second single-drink tab.

The price tag was my introduction to a cold, hard fact of Norway — beer is expensive. Norway's alcohol tax makes its alcohol sales the most expensive in Europe.

It's a little alarming to only be able to drink beers that are at least ten bucks, with many closer to fifteen. With this in mind, I'd recommend Norway's rich culture of craft beer, since "cheap" stuff like Aass (yes, there's a mass-produced Norwegian beer whose name sounds like "ass") will be expensive anyway.

Kroner prices are at least easy to read — just move the decimal point one space to the left if you're used to dollars or euros. For example, 100 Norwegian kroner is a little more than USD$10. Tax is listed in the price, so even if things look expensive, there's no nasty surprises when it comes time to pay.

"I landed in Oslo a few hours ago," I said to the bartender. "Flew in from Chicago."

"Wow!" he laughed nervously. "Welcome!"

Norwegians aren't rude, but most are very no-nonsense and direct. They're not a culture for small talk, especially with people with whom they aren't previously familiar, and they will tell you what they want you to know without beating around the bush. This guy was a little frazzled by having to speak English, but he was nice when you take the cultural barrier into consideration.

"Jeg lærer Norsk," I said that I was learning Norwegian, referencing the handful of months I'd put in on Duolingo. "Jeg snakker ikke godt Norsk." (I don't speak good Norwegian.)

"Deg snakker bra Norsk," he laughed in response, saying my Norwegian was fine — a bold-faced lie, but he was being nice.

You don't have to speak Norwegian as a tourist in Norway, but it's important to learn a few phrases just for goodwill purposes. "Unnskylde" (excuse me) was my most-used word by a considerable margin.

HOW TO HAVE AN ADVENTURE IN SCANDINAVIA

Left:
The bar at Kniven

I finally managed to get the bar tender to tell me his personal favorite offering from Beer Flag. It was "Sargasso," a hoppy Norwegian farmhouse ale named after the Sargasso Sea, a mating ground for eels in the Atlantic. This hard-tasting ale was a great third beer, the strongest of the night.

Drinking my Sargasso amidst the dark decor, I heard the eerie falsetto of King Diamond ring out from the speakers as one of Mercyful Fate's 80s anthems played. Not a Norwegian metal band, they hail from Copenhagen and were a major influence on the later scene of their northern neighbors, making them relevant to the trip.

A group of guys who looked like they were in a band coming in after practice ordered drinks and sat down at a table in the corner. I was three drinks deep, and in Norway, that means a tab nearing forty bucks.

Beer finished, I thanked the bar tender who warmly invited me to return. There wouldn't end up being time, but I had a good evening and some great øl at this outlandish bar — a fine introduction to the wild ride that would be Norway.

Akershus Fortress from across Pipervika Bay

Oslo's East End:
High Ramparts to Helvete

Let me give you some life advice that you can use not only in Norway, but anywhere — don't just have beer for dinner.

But, I'd told myself as I rolled into bed the previous night, *I had that leberkase for lunch!*

That doesn't count, and as I woke up feeling it, I showered and immediately headed out in search of breakfast before starting my day's plans.

A short walk south toward the waterfront made me privy to another fact about the Youngstorget neighborhood — few places were open before 9AM on weekdays. It was a Wednesday, and I was having trouble finding even a coffee shop that was open for breakfast.

Cool wind and blazing sun gave me an early May Oslo weather combo. Despite what you might think about the far north, sunblock is necessary in Norway.

Heading west down Kristian IVs Gate, I finally came across an open coffee shop. It was a Kaffebrenneriet location, a Norwegian chain that serves coffee drinks and sandwiches. The barista, a friendly 20-something blonde woman who seemed excited to use her English skills, rescued me from my self-inflicted lack of nourishment by serving me a cappuccino and a breakfast sandwich.

Breakfast made me feel much better. Energy returned, I walked south down Universitetsgata in the direction of the waterfront.

The next block, the street opened up into the fabulous Palace Park which stretched several long blocks from the royal residence Det Kongelige Slot on the far west end to the parliament building Stortingsbygningen on the east. Built in the 19th Century, Stortingsbygningen has near-continually housed the Norwegian government's main body since, with the notable exception of during the Nazi occupation.

On the park's west side toward the middle was the grandiose Nationaltheatret — a historic theater for stage plays that opened in 1899. An impressive building from the outside and a Norwegian Cultural Heritage Site, its dominating presence and perfect location make it impossible to miss. Norwegian playwright Henrik Ibsen's plays are often associated with the theater, though he died only seven years after it opened with one of his plays as an opening performance. Ibsen was perhaps most famous for writing *Peer Gynt*, which is perhaps even more famous for its musical score. We'll get to that later.

Left:
The National Theater

HOW TO HAVE AN ADVENTURE IN SCANDINAVIA

On the east was the idyllic oasis of Spikersuppa square. It's home to an ice skating rink in the winter, which becomes a pond with fountains in warmer months like the one in which I visited. Greenery and spraying water felt like an aesthetic antidote to the concrete mazes I'd wandered since my arrival. On the far side was a statue of a group of deer amidst a grove.

You're never that far from the wilderness in Norway, but it felt further in Youngstorget. This peaceful locale lessened that feeling.

A woman, apparently a fellow tourist, wandered the square a bit away from me taking her own photos. As I continued to take mine, I noticed that she had turned and stood motionless, face first against a tree trunk — remaining so as I crossed the street toward the south. Was she having a trip, a different kind than the one I was on? Who knows, but it was a pretty strange thing to notice. Whatever was happening on the surface of that tree trunk, it must've been extremely interesting to hold her attention for several whole minutes. Maybe add that to your to-do list in Spikersuppa just to see what she was on about.

25

RAFFAEL CORONELLI

Pipervika waterfront

Down the narrow Rosencrantz gate, the buildings opened. Before me was a part of Oslo for which I'd longed since my arrival — the Oslofjord waterfront.

One can always find their way to the waterfront if they have sight of Rädhuset, the administrative building with two ever-looming red brick towers that marks the point the city opens to the fjord. In front of the Rädhuset was Rädhusplass, an open square filled with statues.

Beyond was the harbor. Boats of all makes and masters floated moored at the end of the fjord. Among them were fjord tour boats, which is probably a good option if you don't have a voyage down Oslofjord planned.

Past the harbor, the fjord-end bay known as Pipervika stretched from Aker Brygge marina on the northwest end to the southwest where loomed my first proper destination of major interest in Oslo — the walled medieval fortress keeping watch at the edge of the city, Akershus Festning.

Akershus' various museums didn't open until 10AM. You're free to walk the grounds before hand, but I wanted to get the whole experience. In the mean time, I took a walk up the opposite end of the Pipervika bay by the marina. Seagulls hopped around the boardwalk, chilly fjord winds blowing in off the water.

HOW TO HAVE AN ADVENTURE IN SCANDINAVIA

Waves lapped gently at the sides of moored boats, as well as some other interesting floating objects.

A hut on a raft extended just off the side of a pier. A sign on it read "saunas / hot tubs". It was the Oslo Fjord Spa, a floating business that allows warm relaxation out on the often-cold waters. Saunas are from Finland, but can be found across Scandinavia. I didn't partake (maybe that's for a potential Finland trip), but the idea of sitting in one on the water of the windy fjord is sort of amusing and may actually be a nice clash of sensations. I'm a big fan of Japanese onsen (hot spring baths), so I'd imagine such a setup would be to my liking if I'd had time to do it.

In the background across the bay, the ramparts of Akershus dominated the view as they had since the Middle Ages. Just over an hour remained until its facilities opened, but I was enjoying my sidetracked stroll and was in no hurry.

At the end of the Aker Brygge peninsula is an island filled with interesting ultramodern architecture. Crossing a short bridge and squeezing between the buildings, I found myself in an open fjordside park filled with art installations. Tjuvholmen Sculpture Park, a small attraction in an idea location, offered a number of strange modern sculptures. Oslo has a rich connection with art history, particularly dealing with the weird and surreal. Tjuvholmen was a fine appetizer for my deep dive into surreal art that afternoon and the following day with two important Norwegian masters of the visually weird.

Right:
"Spalt" by Franz West,
Tjuvholmen Sculpture Park

RAFFAEL CORONELLI

"Eyes" by Louise Bourgeois, with Akershus Fortress in the background

My walk down the Pipervika waterfront had a calming effect, like I'd reached the edge of Oslo's storm cloud and passed to a clear blue sky. The clash of aesthetics on display in the city so far was certainly interesting. I noticed a lot of ice cream shops on the marina end of the bay, which might offer something while enjoying the view.

There was about half an hour to go by the time I made my way back to Rädhusplass, so I decided to grab something to drink in my quest to try the favorite local soft drinks of every country I visit. Ducking into a shop, I perused the shelves and landed on a sizable stock of Solo and Solo Super orange drinks. They reminded me of my favorite orange soft drink in the world, Scotland's mighty Irn Bru. Norwegian Irn Bru was something I couldn't pass up, so I grabbed a Solo Super (the sugar-free variant).

I entered the park around Akershus looking for a place to sample the beverage. To my surprise, I found a statue of Franklin D. Roosevelt. It feels random at first to see a statue of an American president in Scandinavia, but Roosevelt was instrumental in bringing members of the Norwegian Royal Family out of Norway when the Nazis invaded and began their wartime occupation of the country.

HOW TO HAVE AN ADVENTURE IN SCANDINAVIA

The WWII-era United States also provided aid to the Norwegian resistance against the Nazi occupiers. The Norwegian Resistance Museum is located within Akershus, and was one of my destinations for the day.

Taking a seat on a bench near the Roosevelt statue, I faced out at Pipervika and cracked opened my Solo Super. Carbonation and citrus flavors danced across my tastebuds on the way down, immediately reminding me less of Irn Bru and more of San Pellegrino Aranciata. Refreshing and not overly sweet, Solo Super had won me over and would become a go-to for my time in Norway.

When I'd finished my drink, it was time. The fortress awaited. Depositing the empty bottle in a nearby trash can, I walked up the path to the gate.

Several men in modern military uniforms entered ahead of me. Akershus is still administered by Norwegian Military as it's been during the defense of the country through the ages as various invasions from Northern European neighbors have landed on Oslo's shores. Most of it is open to the public and is not restricted, but there are some places you can't go for obvious reasons.

Left:
A restricted military area at Akershus Fortress

RAFFAEL CORONELLI

Akershus Fortress

As I passed through the gate, the bustle of Oslo vanished. I was in a realm of the past, ghosts of distant battles echoing off the stone walls. This is the vibe of visiting a medieval castle, an almost meditative experience if you're there at a sparsely attended time.

Climbing the stairs up to the battlements, I took in the view of Pipervika bay down below. Akershus is situated high on a ridge overlooking the fjord, giving it a perfect vantage point to defend against attackers from the sea. Cannon positions pointed outward, aiming for enemy ships encroaching on the harbor.

In 1716, King Karl XII of Sweden launched a massive surprise invasion at Kristiania (the former name for Oslo) in an attempt to win an advantage over Norway's powerful political partner Denmark to the south.

HOW TO HAVE AN ADVENTURE IN SCANDINAVIA

Akershus battlements over Pipervika

Swedish ships carrying tens of thousands of men entered the Oslofjord and began their attack on the less assuming Scandinavian nation. While Swedish troops swept into the city, the garrison at the impenetrable Akershus Fortress remained reinforced in their position as they fired down on the invaders.

Constant artillery bombardment from Akershus within Kristiania and an inability to move beyond the city thanks to roads being blocked by an uprising of Norwegian civilians forced Karl's forces into retreat. The invasion had failed.

Continuing through the battlements, I took in the main parts of the castle as they were built throughout the Middle Ages. A castle has stood on that spot since around 1300, and has never been taken by force. There's only been one time that an invading army has occupied Akershus, part of the total surrender of Oslo in 1940. For more on that, I'd go to one of the must-visit attractions within the fortress itself — Norway's Resistance Museum.

RAFFAEL CORONELLI

Entry to the Akershus battlements

HOW TO HAVE AN ADVENTURE IN SCANDINAVIA

Admission was 100 kroner, around USD$10, and was worth it. The museum contains countless artifacts and weapons. Detailed dioramas show the battles fought between the Nazis and the Norwegian military, as well as the bombings of Norwegian cities.

Hitler's forces with their manufactured political ideology that conveniently used out-of-context references to Nordic culture had to fight a brutal campaign to take control of Norway with bombardment and aerial battles. The surrender came only when Nazi sympathizers supplanted the Norwegian government with a coup amidst the confusion. That didn't stop the Norwegians who fought the invaders until the Third Reich's demise — a demise they helped bring about.

Among the most important accomplishments of the Norwegian Resistance was the sabotage of the Nazis' heavy water factory in Telemark in 1943. The Nazis planned to use Norwegian facilities to create radioactive material for a singular purpose — the manufacture of an atomic bomb to use against the Allies. One of the "Heroes of Telemark" who thwarted this plan was Knut Haugland, who would later accompany Thor Heyerdahl on the Kon-Tiki expedition in the South Pacific, and would become the first director of Norway's Resistance Museum.

The information presented is invaluable to understanding Norway's relationship with this dark time in history, and how the current Norway is built on liberation from a brutal regime that overtook it.

Akershus took up most of my morning and allowed an aesthetic respite within its walls above urban Oslo. Leaving its impenetrable ramparts behind, I continued east to Bjørvika on the other side of the castle. A modern harbor separated from where I'd spent my morning by the outcropping on which the castle stands, the Bjørvika waterfront is home to two major attractions.

RAFFAEL CORONELLI

The Operahuset and the Munch Museum from across Bjørvika

The first, one of the most iconic pieces of Oslo's modern cityscape, was Operahuset. Oslo's Opera House is exactly what its name suggests, but that won't be your activity there if you visit during the day. Instead, the way to partake in the building is by climbing to the top of it. I have to imagine it's frowned upon to climb the stepped building when it's slippery from rain, snow, or especially ice that would make it extremely dangerous. On a sunny day like the one on which I visited, it's the perfect way to get a vantage point to see the bay, and to experience one of the more original architectural features the city has to offer.

Striking in its blinding white geometric design, Operahuset is covered both in imported Italian Carrera marble and white granite which give it the feeling of a piece of some futuristic Roman forum. Its angled roof rises up from the ground level like an enormous white squall rolling in from the fjord.

Stepping onto the blazing white marble, I began my ascent. Its smooth mountainside doesn't rise at too sharp an angle, but I held my balance carefully so as not to paint the white building with a red streak.

HOW TO HAVE AN ADVENTURE IN SCANDINAVIA

The top of the Operahuset

RAFFAEL CORONELLI

Bjørvika from the Operahuset roof

From the top, I surveyed Bjørvika bay. An interesting sculpture made of jagged glass on a metal frame adorned a small island just offshore. Past the sculpture was a giant ferry that takes passengers to Copenhagen, on which I had a ticket for the following week.

HOW TO HAVE AN ADVENTURE IN SCANDINAVIA

The Munch Museum

On the other side of the Opera House was a rectangular building that warped midway up, its top floors leaning forward like a stack of cards getting ready to fall over. This surreal modern design was adorned with a single word, marking my next destination of the day, one that signaled a deep dive into a strange and fearsome realm — Munch.

That building was the Munch Museum, named for painter Edvard Munch, one of Norway's most influential visual artists.

Again being careful not to smear myself on the tilted roof of Operahuset, I descended and went next door to the Munch. Warped architecture overhead, I entered and headed to the admission desk, depositing my bag in a free locker before passing the ticket gate.

RAFFAEL CORONELLI

"Scream" by Edvard Munch, 1910

HOW TO HAVE AN ADVENTURE IN SCANDINAVIA

Many of Edvard Munch's works display an unstable subconscious; a surreal horror embodied by his most famous painting, "Scream". This darkness of the human condition into which he tapped is emblematic of a facet of Norwegian art — an obsession with the grim and bizarre, reaching into the void and pulling out what lurks below.

"Scream" itself is on display in the museum, albeit in alternating versions. Munch painted several, and a timed apparatus switches out which is shown to the public. If one was out in the open constantly, it would accrue damage due to the materials on which he painted and their reaction to things like the breath of visitors. The universal explosion of existential dread is locked away by a computerized system while another emerges into the open. One by one, the paintings take their turn to scream — as do we all.

Other pieces by Munch are just as evocative. "Blood Waterfall" depicts what its name suggests, a surreal phenomenon from a nightmare world. "Vampyr" shows a woman taking the neck of a bent-over man into her teeth and, uh, munching. (Munch's name sounds like "Moonk" in the Norwegian pronunciation, but let me have that one).

Left:
"Blood Waterfall"
by Edvard Munch
1915-17

RAFFAEL CORONELLI

"Vampyr" by Edvard Munch, 1893

    The museum's collection of paintings are split up into several themed collections on different floors, some of which include works by other painters that share topics and influence in the artistic realms in which Munch dabbled. The museum has a cafe on the ground floor and a restaurant at the top, neither of which I tried. Be warned, you apparently need a reservation to eat in the restaurant. One interesting exhibit displayed artifacts from his home in an attempt to show what life was like for the painter who made such arresting visual works.

HOW TO HAVE AN ADVENTURE IN SCANDINAVIA

As I rode the escalators upward through the various exhibitions, there was one at the top that I was especially anticipating. On the tenth floor of the Munch, a special temporary exhibit ran for the summer of 2022.

It was a selection of paintings by Munch with a special collaboration by Norwegian musical artists inspired by his work, whose genre taps into a similar place of darkness in the psyche. The exhibition was called *Satyricon & Munch*, and indeed, the music created for the exhibition was an original composition by seminal Norwegian Black Metal band Satyricon.

The opening to the gallery room emitted a low, atmospheric guitar tone. The sound grew all-encompassing as I entered. Darkness closed in as the walls opened up to a cavernous space submerged in pitch black. The majesty of Satyricon's epic, 56-minute composition echoed through the hall on a loop. Sounds and melodies of rumbling hyper-distorted guitars, haunting synthesizers, and a menagerie of traditional instruments from cello to theremin swirled into a deep, layered texture meant to be enjoyed while wandering into the exhibition hall at random points (the piece has no discernible beginning or end other than the arbitrary start and stop of the track).

RAFFAEL CORONELLI

"Kiss of Death" by Edvard Munch, 1899

The only real lights in the immense space were spotlights pointing at a series of paintings lining the walls — a selection of Munch's works chosen by the band. Each work related in some way to the band's aesthetic — Norwegian forests, ghoulish figures, strange dreamscapes. Among the art pieces was Munch's "Kiss of Death", which the band had previously featured as the cover art for their more relatively "traditional" album *Deep Calleth Upon Deep*.

After inspecting the paintings close-up, I sat on the row of benches at the far wall to view the installation and listen to more of the progressive track as it wound and twisted through acoustic interludes and down-tuned tremolo riffs. Mesmerizing, hypnotic, transportive, the combination of Munch's artwork and Satyricon's music was a match I was glad to be able to experience in that cavernous space — and only in Norway was it possible.

HOW TO HAVE AN ADVENTURE IN SCANDINAVIA

Norway's music culture is vibrant and storied, from Viking folk songs, to Edvard Grieg, to ambient techno, to Black Metal. The country's most notorious cultural export in recent decades, Norwegian Black Metal has not been an easy thing for many to stomach. Its harsh sonic aesthetic and the ghoulish mystique of the extreme but highly sensationalized antics of young genre musicians when it rose to prominence in the 1990s have made it a hard sell. I'll call it an acquired taste, like a fine hard liquor.

It's an unmistakable product of the region, taking British, American, and other European Heavy Metal and filtering it through repressed Norwegian resentment that long simmered under a reserved surface. It has a strong element of deranged camp in its most theatrical acts. Most importantly, if you ask me, the music rocks.

It also hits that same cultural spot, that very Norwegian fascination with the dark and the strange, that Munch captured in his paintings. That such an exhibition as *Satyricon & Munch* would exist even temporarily in a major and globally respected art museum is a testament to its success as a medium.

Somewhere along the line since it was deemed too frightening for mass consumption in the 1990s, Norwegian Black Metal has become part of Norway's draw for the musically adventurous and one of its contemporary cultural institutions. If a goal of the early scene was to quake the foundations of what reserved Norwegian attitudes considered acceptable, things like this are a sign that they entirely succeeded — but it also shows how much sense it all makes in the grand scheme of Norwegian art.

Satyricon & Munch ran through the end of August, 2022. While you won't be able to see it at this point, Satyricon's composition for the exhibit is available to listen to as an album fittingly titled *Satyricon & Munch*. All parties involved put together a phenomenal exhibit — a great sign for what the museum is willing to do.

RAFFAEL CORONELLI

To fully immerse in this type of music that had compelled me for years, there was one more spot I needed to hit that afternoon, just a walk inland in the Grønland neighborhood. Moving away from the waterfront, I headed across the Nordenga bridge to Schweigaards gate.

A storefront on the northeast side of the street was covered in posters and metal memorabilia. Across the top of the doorway hung a sign that read, in splattered lettering, "Neseblod". It was time to descend into Helvete.

Neseblod Records occupies a space that previously belonged to another record store called Helvete, which served as a hangout for prominent bands in the early 90s. It was owned and operated by a guitarist who went by the name Euronymous until his untimely murder in 1993.

Metal memorabilia completely encircled me as soon as I stepped through the door. Every inch of Neseblod's top floor (and much of its bottom floor) is covered in metal records, cassettes, CDs, and merchandise. It's like entering a shrine to the esoteric music genre, one that still stands over unhallowed ground.

I wanted to have a look around the store itself for some subterranean musical discoveries, but first, there was something I needed to see. A sign over the spiral staircase to the basement read "no bags", prompting me to leave my backpack with the friendly owner at the checkout counter. Pushing an Immortal t-shirt out of the way like a cobweb in Castle Dracula, I descended the stairs.

While it is a record store, Neseblod is also a "museum" of Black Metal. Shelves are stocked with original rare demos and unique pieces of the genre's history. Some items are signed by musicians; Fenriz from the influential bands Darkthrone and Isengard maintains a relationship with the store, bestowing his signature to a number of releases I saw on the shelves.

HOW TO HAVE AN ADVENTURE IN SCANDINAVIA

Neseblod Records storefront

45

RAFFAEL CORONELLI

The real draw to Neseblod, however, isn't just what's on sale — but what's beneath it. Searching the basement for a minute with the help of a few signs with arrows, I found the semi-hidden doorway. On the other side, there were no shelves, no furnishings — just tan concrete with atmosphere like an ancient tomb. Stepping inside, the air grew colder.

These chambers and passageways were where members and cohorts of bands like Mayhem, Emperor, Immortal, Satyricon, and Darkthrone would gather in the genre's early days. Now this dungeon cave system echoed with their enshrined legacy as I wound deeper into the caverns beneath Oslo.

A poster hung on the wall depicting a live photo of one of the genre's icons, Abbath. The Bergen native fronted the band Immortal before forming his own band named after himself, delivering driving guitar riffs and helping establish Norwegian Black Metal's campier side with his theatrical flair.

Around the corner, the tomb's treasure increased. A massive banner emblazoned with the logo of Mayhem, the late store founder's near-mythical band, was draped from wall to wall — a backdrop used on stage in early live shows. Crates of artifacts related to the early scene lay about.

> Welcome to the chamber of death and horror, to the land of the Vikings, to a land of pure evil, to a place where only death is real. You are invited to pure fucking MAYHEM!

From an early 90s Mayhem flyer in the basement of Neseblod Records

HOW TO HAVE AN ADVENTURE IN SCANDINAVIA

One more open door led into the final inner sanctum.

A coffin lay in the corner. During his short but genre-shaping tenure, undead/Dracula-loving Mayhem vocalist Per "Dead" Ohlin would sometimes use a coffin in his visceral act. Much has been made of his own tragic end, often tastelessly, but I prefer to remember the art for which he lived and the extreme vocal sound he pioneered. I don't think this particular prop was his, but he came to mind when I saw it.

On the other side of the room stood a candelabra topped with an inverted pentagram. Scrawled on the wall next to it as if a curse from the dark past to mark the place's purpose and occupants through the aeons were two words.

Right:
The author of this book with an inscription by early 90s-era musicians (possibly Euronymous) in the basement of Neseblod Records

RAFFAEL CORONELLI

Neseblod Records' racks

HOW TO HAVE AN ADVENTURE IN SCANDINAVIA

I returned to the topside caverns to engage in my other reason for visiting, to look for some new-to-me Black Metal to take home. Neseblod has a staggering selection of both CDs and vinyl records, but I was carrying my goods back to the US and needed easily packable items. Thus, I went straight for the tapes. Cassette might be the ideal format to listen to Black Metal, anyway. Something about tapes' rickety playing mechanism and their archaic nature makes a genre release on the medium feel like some cursed artifact dug out of the ground in a forest somewhere.

A prominent display in the corner showed CDs from Trelldom and Gorgoroth, bands with whom the enigmatic frontman Gaahl performed prior to his current band Gaahls Wyrd. This would not be the last sign of Gaahl on the trip.

Careful not to knock over precarious stacks of tapes, I fingered through the releases. My selection criteria weren't too strict, mostly going off of tapes' vibes.

One cassette read, "No contact with the band! Limited to 500 copies!" No contact? What happened to them? What happens to *you* if you contact them? This was clearly a cursed item and I had to buy it.

More satisfying was a tape from Myrholt, hailing from Norway's Nordland region. The cassette was quite the find, a 50-copy pressing of 2017 album *Med Samme Nål, Under Samme Måne*. This release had the meat-and-potatoes Black Metal goods — icy tremolo guitar melodies, atmospheric lo-fi interludes, echoing howls of the vocalist. The subject matter, reflected in some nice photography in the cassette's booklet, is of the Norwegian wilderness and nature. The tape is too limited to track down at this point, but the artist does have it available for streaming online.

With the amount of clothing Neseblod sells, you may want to buy a shirt. They sell their own shirts brandished with the store logo, which makes a nice souvenir.

The rack was out of shirts in my size, but the owner went to the back to retrieve one when I told him.

Between my purchases and the incomparable experience of visiting, Neseblod delivered on its cult status and was a highlight of my time in Oslo.

Spoils of the caverns' treasures in my bag, I headed up Grønlandsleiret in the direction of the hotel, northwest through the Grønland neighborhood. There's one more piece of trivia for fans of Black Metal on this street around the corner from Neseblod.

Norwegian metal titans Dimmu Borgir did the initial recording of their 1996 opus *Stormblåst* in a now-defunct Oslo studio on Grønlandsleiret. The band were so unhappy with how the album sounded in the then-typical lo-fi Norwegian Black Metal recording style that they moved their next album's recording to Sweden and later redid *Stormblåst* in its entirety there. This marked the beginning of the end for the primitive recording aesthetic associated with prominent early genre releases, though some bands would continue to seek it out on purpose as an aesthetic choice. Mass-listener-friendly decisions like this made Dimmu Borgir objects of outcry from purists, but the band's international superstardom in the mid-2000s put Norwegian music on the map for a lot of Ozzfest-attending, *Headbangers' Ball*-watching American teenagers at the time — the author of this book included.

The street is also home to Rock In, a bar I only saw from the outside. Rock In is a cheaper but similarly-themed alternative to Kniven.

Immediately noticeable in Grønland is that it's now a middle eastern immigrant neighborhood. Stores, restaurants, and the omnipresent kabob shops are run by Oslo's vibrant population of middle eastern descent. There were plenty of options for that sort of food, if you're in the mood for it. That evening, I had other meal plans for which I wanted to have an appetite.

HOW TO HAVE AN ADVENTURE IN SCANDINAVIA

After dropping off my bag at the hotel, I headed out to dinner. I was about to make my long-delayed first foray into traditional Norwegian cuisine. For that, I'd head to an older restaurant that's been doing it for decades.

Located on Kristian IVs gate (which to the southeast is called Grensen, because Oslo streets are just like that) on the ground floor of the Hotel Bondeheimen, is Kaffistova. A traditional Norwegian restaurant, Kaffistova has been serving home style Norwegian food since 1901. Entering into the nicely decorated interior, I began the ordeal of figuring out how exactly one orders.

Kaffistova is the type of restaurant where one would assume a waiter would come to your table. Instead, people order at a counter before a waiter brought them their food.

After looking over the menu, I went up to the counter to place my order for elgkarbonade (moose patties) and a glass of Gammel Opland, one of Norway's most popular aquavits. While the waiter does indeed bring your food when it's ready, I had to go up to a counter to get my aquavit. To be honest, I found the service unhelpful and the whole process confounding. Luckily, that was canceled out by the meal itself.

First, a primer on aquavit. From my first sip of Gammel Opland, my tastebuds delighted to a semi-sweet (but not sugary) caraway liquor as it rolled back across my tongue. Aquavit is, in the simplest terms, vodka that tastes good. Distilled from potatoes or grain, just like vodka, it's infused with herbs and spices that give it its signature flavors. Each aquavit has different combinations of ingredients and thus tastes a little bit different.

Danish aquavit is the original, a clear liquor that tastes more of alcohol and strong caraway. Swedish aquavit is sweeter, but closer to the Danish kind in coloration. Norwegian aquavit is slightly more amber in color and soft in flavor, which comes from how it's aged.

The original Norwegian style aquavit was Danish liquor stored in barrels at sea that aged longer than intended during an extended voyage. When the Norwegians finally got to drinking it, it had matured into the flavorful variety produced on purpose in Norway today.

What's especially nice about aquavit is how you drink it — a single, small glass before and during a meal. This isn't a drink for binging, though the flavor certainly tempts. Danish and Swedish aquavits are served chilled, while Norwegian ones are served at room temperature. My journey through different types of this Scandinavian liquor would continue throughout the trip, making it one of my new favorite beverages.

The food was delicious as well. Venison is a big part of traditional Norwegian cuisine, much more so than any other red meat. This stems from the country's local fauna. Deer, moose, and further north, reindeer are much more common than other large mammals.

The moose patties were served with mushrooms, root vegetables, potatoes, and lingonberry jam. These are all common local ingredients for Norway, and would turn up again and again in the traditional food I ate there. These were the sumptuous flavors of land-based Nordic cuisine, the food of Viking farmers and the northern woods.

My first full day in Oslo was packed and immensely satisfying. Whatever reservations I've had about navigating the city were nullified by the things I got to do there, like Kaffistova's ordering process by the food they serve. Returning to the hotel, it didn't take long to fall asleep.

The next day would be one of diving deeper into Norway's history.

HOW TO HAVE AN ADVENTURE IN SCANDINAVIA

Elgkarbonade (moose patties) at Kaffistova

A medieval loft at the Norsk Folkemuseum

Oslo's West End:
The City's Hoard

While I'd visited the Resistance Museum and the Munch on my first day, Oslo has a concentration of incredible collections in its West End borough of Frogner that deserve a day trip to the other side of the city to see.

First, I downloaded the Oslo "Ruter" app for bus tickets and bought a 24 hour transit pass. That taken care of, I headed out for the all-important breakfast.

A brief research session looking for places that were open before leaving the hotel led me to La Belle Flør, a charming combination cafe and plant shop that offers an array of breakfast sandwiches and coffee.

As I sat eating a nice egg sandwich with micro greens and sipping a cappuccino, my eyes drifted out the window to the imposing architectural form that loomed across the street. La Belle Flør is situated just across from St. Olav's Cathedral.

There are a number of cathedrals in Oslo, but this one is notable for being named after the Christian Viking King Olav, canonized as a saint because he brought Christianity to all of Norway at the edge of a sword. Scandinavia's relationship with Christianity's arrival and its supplanting of the Norse religion by brutal force are a part of the region's history associated with certain cultural scars.

RAFFAEL CORONELLI

Left:
St. Olav's Cathedral
from the window of La Belle Flør

St. Olav's Neo-Gothic cathedral built in the 19th Century is a historic piece of Oslo's cityscape that's worth a look, though it's also worth considering the symbolic dissonance of its namesake. I'd be seeing a genuine piece of this turbulent 11th-century transition period later that day, making my breakfast in the cathedral's shadow an interesting primer.

Post-breakfast, I went west up St. Olav's Gate. This was the direction of the Sentrum, Oslo's beautiful city center I'd passed through the previous morning, where I'd catch my bus to the west end. On the way, I noticed a hilltop park, Halfdan Kjerulfs plass.

Halfdan Kjerulfs plass is a small respite from the city below. Elevated on its hill, it sits next to the Sentrum covered in colorful, patterned flower gardens in the warmer spring months. I sat on a park bench enjoying a Solo Super that I'd bought from a nearby convenience store, overlooking the Kulturhistorik Museum.

If you have time, the Kulturhistorik Museum has Viking era artifacts that are by all accounts well worth checking out. It was unfortunately still closed at the time I passed, and I already had five other museums on the agenda for the day to which I needed to get.

After my brief stop, I continued southwest across the Sentrum park to Sortingsgata, a wide boulevard with bus stops for the Nationaltheatret (from the previous day).

HOW TO HAVE AN ADVENTURE IN SCANDINAVIA

Nationaltheatret is the stop at which to get on the bus going west to Bygdøy.

Bus and tram tickets in Oslo are most conveniently handled on an app, which is easier to figure out and pay on than some others I tried to use on the trip. Hold your pass on your phone screen up to a reader when you get on — or, as long as you've paid and you have the pass on your phone, just get on the bus. This honor system method is what most Norwegians practice and was a major moment of culture shock. The bus rumbled and we were off to the unexplored side of the city.

Starting in the 19th Century, the West End of Oslo has been home to a more economically elite populace, while the East End (the area east of the Sentrum) is more working class and has cheaper real estate. Built around industry, the part in which I'd spent my time so far does benefit from the universally high quality of life throughout the country, but still experiences the divide. The West End, particularly the Frogner bureau, is home to the most expensive residential real estate in all of Norway.

This was immediately apparent as the bus headed west. Greenery was more plentiful and buildings had more of a Haussmann architectural style like one would see in Paris. The city felt less claustrophobic and more high-end.

There are a number of hotels in the West End, some of them quite affordable. If you'd rather do the opposite of what I did, you can centralize your stay in the Frogner neighborhood and make a day trip to the East End of the city. Either approach would work with the itinerary of this book, since I spent one full day on either side of town.

Frogner bureau was where I'd localized this day's activities. Within it was one particular geographic spot that housed some of Oslo's most impressive collections.

Bygdøy is sometimes called Oslo's "museum island," though it's not an island at all and is actually peninsula. Its name comes from the five museums it houses.

RAFFAEL CORONELLI

The Vikingskipshuset is home to an impressive collection of Viking ships, as the name suggests. Unfortunately, it was undergoing an extensive renovation during my visit and was closed. I had another Viking ship museum on the agenda for Denmark, so I could put off that experience for later.

Among the other four is the Norsk Folkemuseum (also called the Norwegian Museum of Cultural History), which is more of an outdoor architecture park featuring traditional buildings relocated from other parts of Norway. Before that, I'd head to the tip of the peninsula at the edge of the fjord for a trio of them focused on maritime and Norway's grand history of sea voyages.

Getting off the bus at the Fredriksborg stop, I followed the winding downhill road one kilometer through the forested neighborhood at the tip of Bygdøy. At the end of it, the trees cleared and there stood a row of buildings at the edge of the sea.

Right to left from the direction of arrival, they were the boxy Norwegian Maritime Museum, the massive pair of triangular hangers that constitute the Fram Museum, and the smaller Kon-Tiki museum. I had a moment before they opened, so I walked past to the waterfront to take in the view of the Oslofjord from this ideal vantage point.

Water lapped at the shore below. Various maritime artifacts from the nearby museum lined the oceanside parkway in outdoor displays, including several small boats, an anchor, and a naval mine. There was also a dock where one could catch a ferry to and from the Opera House, though the timing didn't work out for me and the bus was cheaper. Out on the fjord, the lumbering DFDS *Pearl Seaways* ferry from Copenhagen sailed in to port. Morning sun glinted off the water on a perfect, cloudless day. Those few minutes on the edge of the fjord offered serenity and the perfect way to get into the mindset of the sea before the ocean voyage-themed material I was about to encounter.

HOW TO HAVE AN ADVENTURE IN SCANDINAVIA

If you only go to one of the three museums, make it the Fram. You don't have to choose unless you're terribly pressed for time, as an affordable combination ticket to all three is available at any of their admission desks, which was the choice I went with.

Upon entering the Fram Museum, the lower temperature and cool blue lighting within weren't the only things that immediately struck my attention. A gargantuan ship's bow loomed across the entire main hall housing the museum's main attraction and namesake.

Left:
The bow of the Fram

RAFFAEL CORONELLI

The deck of the Fram

HOW TO HAVE AN ADVENTURE IN SCANDINAVIA

Launched in 1892, *Fram* was the ship of several noted Norwegian Arctic and Antarctic explorers — first Fridtjof Nansen, then Otto Sverdrup, and finally Roald Amundsen. Built exclusively for use in the polar regions by Norwegian shipbuilders who knew what it took to cross into those icy waters, the ship was a lumbering, ice-breaking wooden vessel with room for enough stocks to last years — one of the last great accomplishments of the wooden ship era.

Museum exhibits lined the rims around it. I took my time with them as they told the stories of the expeditions in which the ship took part. Other exhibits dealt with arctic animals, the arctic landscape, and the sailors' means of disembarking and exploring the ice. There was even a display dedicated to the type of aquavit they brought with them, a specially dedicated shipment of Linie, which I'd try in a few days. Led around to the deck's entrance on the third level, it was time to board.

Wood creaked as I stepped on the deck of a ship that had traversed the top and bottom of the Earth. Imposing masts towered overhead, the deck itself a sprawling field of enforced wooden boards.

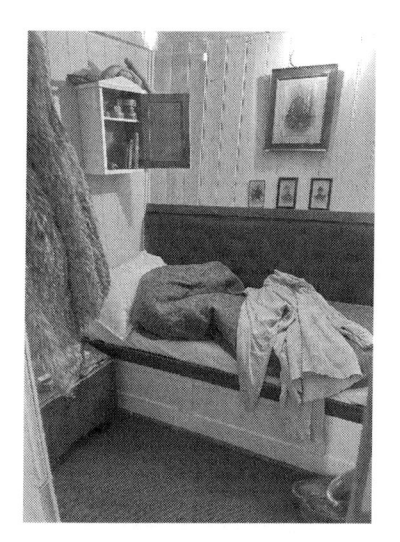

Descending inside, the cramped cabins went on into the ship's interior. Places where the sailors slept, ate, gathered, and worked with the mechanisms of the ship were fully restored and presented as they were in the period. Amundsen's tiny quarters had all the comforts of a home he'd inhabited for years on end.

Left: Amundsen's cabin

61

RAFFAEL CORONELLI

This was a vessel of those who lived to explore, who went on dangerous journeys into the northern unknown. It was incomparable to my own just-for-fun adventure, but it set a tone and foreshadowed my voyages to come — into the Norwegian Arctic, and then south to Denmark by ship. If nothing else, it was a wonderful frame of reference.

A separate hanger connected by an underground passageway was home to the *Gjøa*, the ship in which Amundsen sailed through the Northwest Passage. This smaller ship was impressive in its own right, and similarly prepared for boarding with exhibits outside and inside it that displayed its workings and the context of the expedition.

Right:
The Gjøa

HOW TO HAVE AN ADVENTURE IN SCANDINAVIA

The way these two ships were presented was the closest one could get to sailing on them. The Fram Museum is unmissable, even if you have limited time in the West End.

Heading next door, I used the second part of my triple-admission ticket for the Norwegian Maritime Museum. The more general exhibitions inside dealt with smaller (sometimes miniaturized) examples of Norway's expansive maritime history. A special exhibit displayed Norwegian paintings of sailing over the centuries. Models of all manner of ships from wooden masted, to trawlers, to oceangoing ferries told the story Norway's shipbuilding progression. Outside the museum, the tall mast ship *Svanen* stood docked, having sailed in the Norwegian merchant fleet at the turn of the 20th Century.

Right: The author of this book with the Svanen

RAFFAEL CORONELLI

On the opposite side of the Fram Museum was the last item on my three-part ticket — the Kon-Tiki Museum. Considered one of the great sea adventures of the modern era, the *Kon-Tiki* sailed in 1947 from Peru to French Polynesia with a crew lead by Thor Heyerdahl who'd just gotten out of the horrors of World War II.

HOW TO HAVE AN ADVENTURE IN SCANDINAVIA

The basis for the expedition was mostly nonsense, to recreate an imagined ancient voyage from South America to Polynesia by those who would populate the islands. In history, Polynesians migrated from East Asia and are descended from the native populations of Taiwan and the Philippines, rather than from the opposite direction. Nonetheless, the adventure proved to a global audience how far a traditional Polynesian ship could go, and gave some newly postwar Norwegian lads an excuse to have a wild time in the South Seas.

The Kon-Tiki Museum also contained the ship *Ra II* from a similar expedition in which Heyerdahl attempted an Atlantic crossing in an Egyptian style ship from Morocco to the Caribbean. Like with the *Kon-Tiki*, there's not any historical precedence for this voyage, but Heyerdahl and his crew did make it to Barbados.

One gets the impression from all of this that Heyerdahl's crackpot theories about ancient migration were secondary to a desire to go on long, ocean-crossing trips on weird, custom-built boats. The ships themselves were very cool to see in person.

The seafaring history of Norway had left its impression and gotten me ready for the boats I'd be taking later on in the trip. Inland from the tip of the peninsula, I headed toward the last stop on Bygdøy.

Opposite left:
The Kon-Tiki

RAFFAEL CORONELLI

The Norse Folkemuseum, or Norwegian Cultural History Museum, is the largest on Bygdøy. It's a sprawling outdoor space built by King Oscar II (the guy on the King Oscar sardine cans) to preserve traditional examples of Norwegian architecture from across Norway.

After paying admission at the entrance, I was given a map of the grounds. It's split up into areas, sort of like theme park "lands", based on different regions of Norway. Unlike a theme park, it's all real architecture.

The notion that they're all "original", though, is a little bit of misnomer. Over time, pieces of these buildings have been replaced and retouched out of necessity. Wood simply doesn't last as long as other building materials. It decays, becomes unstable, and makes the buildings structurally unsound if it's not kept up in a controlled environment — and outdoors in Norway is anything but a controlled environment. I mention this in case you're wondering how some of these wood-built pieces are able to survive over a thousand years. The answer is that expert craftspeople perform regular touch-ups.

I saw one such touch-up being performed in real time as I passed the Jæren area of the park, a district on Norway's southwest coast. Workmen adjusted wood paneling on a grass-roofed house. It appeared similar to a sod house, though its overall material was white-painted wood with only the top covered in grass — a rural Nordic design feature. Sod and grass cover the roof protect from the rainy weather in southwest Norway, carried up by the Gulf Stream. This served as a reminder before I headed west to the notoriously rainy Bergen.

Other areas represented in the park included Telemark, Enerhaugen, Hallingdal, Østlandet, Sognefjord (where I would travel in a few days), Trøndlag, Østerdal, and Finnmark.

HOW TO HAVE AN ADVENTURE IN SCANDINAVIA

A farm building from Hallingdal in the Norsk Folkemuseum

The section dedicated to houses from the eastern Hallingdal area had one of especially interesting significance. According to a plaque near the summer farmhouse that was moved to the museum from the town of Bjørnebergstølen, the house is allegedly where the Norwegian folktale "Fanitullen" took place.

I stepped up to the house and scanned the dark main room. Despite the bright sun that day, light had trouble reaching the interior by the design of the windows, if not by some notion that it was not a place where light should go. The floor was empty, but the walls had ornate carvings on some of the boards. The room was big enough to imagine a party having taken place there with home-brewed beer, multiple nights of reveling, and a fateful argument.

Such a line of thought takes us back three centuries...

HOW TO HAVE AN ADVENTURE IN SCANDINAVIA

Fanitullen

A Norwegian folktale,
retold and embellished by Raffael Coronelli

The story goes that in 1724, at a peasant wedding in a rural town in Hallingdal, two men got into a fight. It could've been about anything, but was likely exacerbated by the fact that the party had been going for days with no break in consuming the host's øl.

Amidst the reveling, two belligerent drunks announced their brawl to begin, much to the party's delight. With bare-knuckle boxing for entertainment, the crowd decided to gift the fight's winner another beer.

Weddings in this era had a toast master, someone who would've been in charge of celebratory drinks. The man responsible for this at the wedding quickly realized he would have to be the one to retrieve the reward. Careful not to trip over his feet as he downed his own drink, he left the chaos and cheering of the fight to retrieve the prize from the cellar where resided the beer barrels — and, beyond his knowledge, something else.

Wooden steps creaked as he descended into the gloomy basement. His lit lantern threw illumination onto only the closest walls. Sounds from the party above faded.

Despite initial appearances, he wasn't alone.

In the shadows, atop a beer barrel, there sat a shape. Its silhouette could've been some piece of debris thrown into the cellar for storage — but what was it doing perched atop a barrel that had seen such heavy recent use? Two fiery glints peered out from it, watching him.

"Who goes there?" he demanded, holding out his lantern to cast illumination on this strange party guest.

RAFFAEL CORONELLI

The lantern's warm light revealed the shape in detail. It was a man, taller than average, with long, spindly limbs. His face had sharp, uncanny features; high, pointy brows above sunken-in eyes surrounded by dark circles that contrasted the burning pupils at their centers. His skin complexion was otherwise pale, made to look a shade of red by the lantern's flame. In his long arms he held a violin that he tuned, though he held it in a strange and incorrect position — upright, strings facing out from his chest.

"Just I," the creature replied, voice calm and crooning like a song.

Drunk, the man decided that he was seeing things and that this was a perfectly normal party guest distorted by some trick of his vision.

"Do you know how to play?" he asked, skeptical at the unconventional way the violin was being held.

"Why yes," the creature smiled. "Would you like to hear a tune?"

"Why not?" the man agreed, having momentarily forgotten why he'd come down to the cellar and finding this guest most interesting.

Finished tuning the instrument, the creature held out the violin — still in a strange position in which the man had never seen the instrument used. Then, he began to play.

The tune wound its way around a deceptively happy melody with something off just below the surface, like an angry person smiling too hard. It frightened and enticed. The man shivered at its uncanny intervals. It ended with a sound that, according to the 19th century poem by Jørgen Moe that retold the story a century later, was the sound of "mannefall" — which translates from Norwegian as "falling men," "casualties," or "slaughter." A simpler translation could be "death," but the Norwegian wording implies a warlike or murder scenario; a violent death, like a man being killed in a fight.

HOW TO HAVE AN ADVENTURE IN SCANDINAVIA

The party's toast master was aghast. He'd never heard anything like it.

"Where did you learn that?" he asked, wondering where such music played in such a manner had originated.

"It matters not," it said, "but remember it well."

The music had finished, but its notes still crawled up the man's back, haunting his thoughts.

"I shall," he whispered.

Then a commotion sounded from the top of the stairs, and he remembered the beer. He'd come down into the cellar to retrieve a beer to give to the fight's winner.

"You'll have to excuse me," he said. "I need to—"

"Of course," the creature smiled, moving his leg out of the way of the tap, clunking its hoof against the wood.

The man stopped. Indeed, its legs ended in hooves.

It wasn't his drunken state. It wasn't a distortion. The inhumanity of his entertainer was no longer in question.

The creature's grin grew wider. The final bars of the Devil's tune wound through the man's memory as he gazed upon the face of evil. In that moment, he knew its intent and its infernal identity.

Falling over himself, the man scrambled up the stairs. Something pulled at his back, made his feet weigh heavier, holding him from running faster. The creature laughed a guttural, echoing laugh, toying with him. Then it released and he burst out through the cellar door, slamming it shut behind him.

He'd never gotten the beer. He didn't need it now.

One of the two fighters lay on the floor, restrained by several other men, face red with anger and spattered viscera. Next to him was the body of his opponent.

Knife wounds covered the dead man's torso, the vicinity drenched in blood. The fight had turned to murder. In that house, much to the amusement of their guest, the partygoers had been spellbound by the Devil.

RAFFAEL CORONELLI

This delightful tale from which I've just entertained you with my own retelling has passed down through three centuries. The Devil making people do things is always a convenient excuse for, say, killing a man in a drunken fight. I do love some good esotericism, though, and "Fanitullen" is an excellent horror story.

The tale was the basis for a piece of traditional folk music, also called "Fanitullen." This violin piece has no known composer, and is said to have been inspired by the one played by Satan himself. It comes with a warning not to play it around drunk people, lest the music influence them to kill each other — which seems more like cheeky dark humor than a genuine issue. Let it be known that the fine tradition of messing with people while playing devil music has been around in Norway for at least three hundred years.

Peering into the dim interior of the Bjørnebergstølen farm house, I contemplated the events said to have transpired there. The murder, the music, the presence of evil. This bare, unlit wooden building was where the terror unfolded.

Satan's murder house isn't the most ornate or spectacular piece in the Norsk Folkemuseum, but it is one of the most notable for its associated story alone. For something with more visual splendor, I'd cross to the other side of the park.

In the northwest corner of the Norsk Folkemuseum stood its most famous attraction. It required following a path up a hill, through a small forest, and to a clearing where loomed a towering specter. First visible through the trees, its pointed peak stood like a tall, cloaked figure. In the clearing, it came into full view.

Steep thatched roofs point toward a jagged, blade-like point tipped with dragon heads and several prominently-placed crosses.

HOW TO HAVE AN ADVENTURE IN SCANDINAVIA

Gol Stave Church

Gol Stave Church originally resided in Hallingdal, the same region as Satan's murder house. Built initially in the 12th Century, its wooden structure decayed from exposure to harsh Norwegian winters for the better part of a millennium until King Oscar II purchased the building and moved it to his open air museum in the 1880s. The only parts that survived the move were pieces of the alter and interior decorations. The outside was reconstructed with then-modern techniques at the new location, and is still maintained by the museum.

RAFFAEL CORONELLI

Built like ships by King Olav's Christian Vikings, Norway's stave churches have an intimidating presence reminiscent of the time in which they originated. These churches were made by shipbuilders, and look the part down to the dragon heads that might've gone on the bow of a longship.

There's another reason stave churches had a look unique from Christian buildings further south. Their design was likely inspired by a different Nordic building.

In 2020, in the town of Ørsta in western Norway, archeologists including Søren Diinhoff from the University of Bergen unearthed the 1,200-year-old foundations of a "godhouse" — a temple to the Norse gods. Its foundation revealed the base of a tower at its center, to which its roof might've sloped up just like a stave church. This building predates the earliest churches in Norway, but shows the beginnings of their architectural style. These godhouses did not survive into the modern era, as they were razed by the 11th Century government that sought to enforce Christianity in the populace and purge the old ways. As reported by Tom Metcalfe in an October 2020 LiveScience article, this godhouse's foundations were accompanied by buried figures of Odin, Thor, and Freyr, suggesting the temple's dedication to them and possibly other gods.

Right:
An open door from inside Gol Stave Church

HOW TO HAVE AN ADVENTURE IN SCANDINAVIA

It's somewhat ironic that the only frame of reference to what a Norse godhouse might've looked like is the thing that supplanted it, but this is the nature of architectural evolution. Every design has roots in something else. The godhouse itself was, according to Diinhoff, inspired by Viking interaction with southern cultures that already had Christian basilicas. Prior, the Norse preferred to perform outdoor rituals.

Aside from the crosses that adorn it periodically, the intricate decorations on Gol Stave Church are purely Nordic in aesthetic and do not depict biblical imagery. The "portal" entranceway, possibly the most impressive piece of art on the church, is a super-ornate aesthetic design that stems from Viking art and is meant to signify passage into another realm. It's easy to imagine these on old Norse buildings.

The stave church was a uniquely Norwegian experience. The forest outside felt blended into its wooden forms as much as the period of violent cultural upheaval in which the building originated. It would not be the last of these buildings I'd encounter.

Left:
Portal arch on Gol Stave Church

RAFFAEL CORONELLI

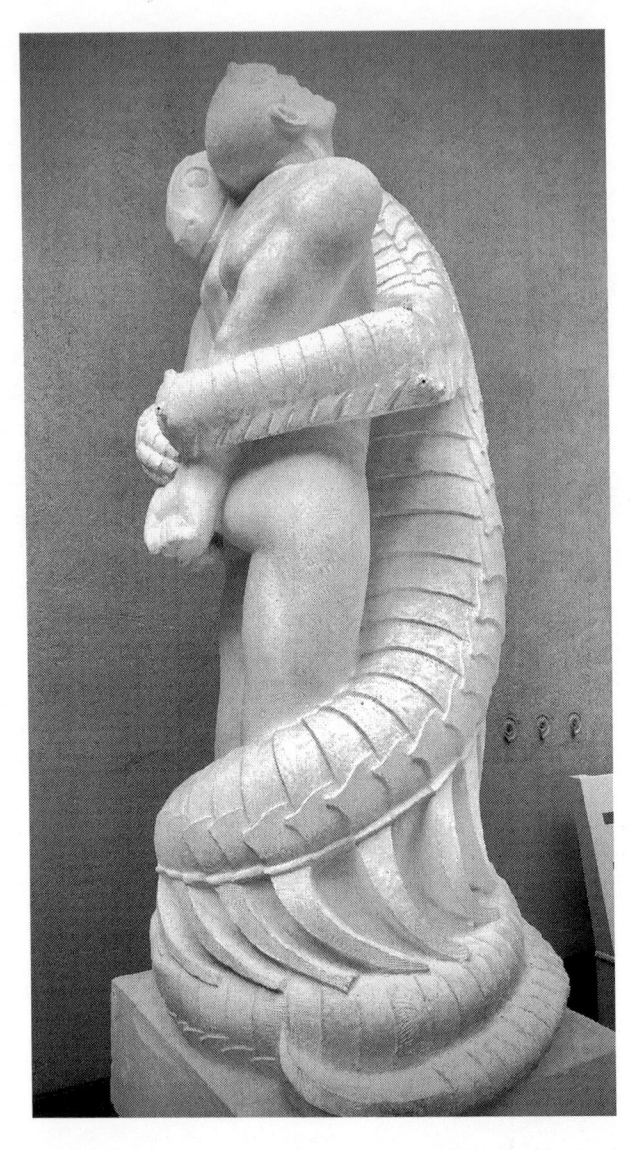

Statue of a dragon creature embracing a man by Gustav Vigeland

HOW TO HAVE AN ADVENTURE IN SCANDINAVIA

On the bus out of Bygdøy, I headed just north to the center of the Frogner neighborhood, to an unmissable section of Frogner Park that's home to a vast collection of works by one of Norway's most interesting artists. When spending any amount of time in Oslo's West End, this is not to be missed.

Occupying the same period at the turn of the 20th Century as Edvard Munch, Gustav Vigeland tapped into the same surreal and occasionally pitch dark realm, though he did it in a completely different medium — sculpture. Vigeland was a supremely gifted sculptor of the human form in lifelike anatomical accuracy. What he did with it was the imagery of a bizarre dream. Impressively, the Vigeland Sculpture Park is all one carefully planned, unified nightmare of which he was the architect.

Heading into Vigeland Sculpture Park from the bus, an idyllic city park turned to a realm of the uncanny as an increasingly strange array of sculptures surrounded me. From the entrance, Vigeland's motif of humans arranging themselves in physically impossible formations became apparent. One of his more famous pieces was in this section, an extremely angry toddler throwing a temper tantrum. This was but a foreshadowing of the baby war to come.

77

RAFFAEL CORONELLI

Statue of a man fighting babies ("Genii") by Gustav Vigeland

My favorite of Vigeland's sculptures and one of the funniest pieces of imagery I've ever seen is the statue of the man fighting the babies. Located on the northwest side of the bridge at the center of the park, this sculpture shows a grown man in the nude (as all of Vigeland's people are) fending off an attack by powerful, vicious, gravity-defying babies. What is the motive of the babies? Just how powerful are they to need him to fend them off with the full use of his martial prowess?

Whether it's an image from an absurd dream, pure absurdism, or some type of symbolic work which Vigeland didn't explain is up to the viewer. I'm glad there's no explanation or context, as this statue is amazing on its own terms and deserves to be taken at face value. The relentless baby attack and the man fending them off speaks to each of us differently. At some point, in some way, we are all the man fighting the babies.

HOW TO HAVE AN ADVENTURE IN SCANDINAVIA

Intense combat between man and babies
at Vigeland Sculpture Park

RAFFAEL CORONELLI

The Column by Gustav Vigeland at Vigeland Sculpture Park

HOW TO HAVE AN ADVENTURE IN SCANDINAVIA

Vigeland's nightmare wonderland led northward through the park to a culmination. Like a massive Egyptian temple, a grandiose monument arose. At its center was an obelisk made of human bodies swarming and writhing over each other as they climbed skyward.

Among the humans were some monsters of various designs, from dragons to crustaceans. They engaged in activities with humans, from grappling to embracing.

I enjoyed Vigeland's sculptures in their context-less absurdity, but I had to know what the guy was on about. For that, I crossed the street to the Vigeland Muset.

Located just across from the park, the museum offers a much more in-depth look at who Vigeland was and his process of creating his magnum opus, the park dedicated to his sculptures. It details his planning stages of the park, from miniature versions to early full-sized sculpts.

It's also a curated collection of his works, including his most famous piece outside the park — "Hel". This carved relief depicts a realm of human misery and, like Munch's "Scream", the darkness of existence. "Hel" hasn't been seen as much in popular culture, though the power of its imagery is no less arresting.

"Hel" by Gustav Vigeland

RAFFAEL CORONELLI

Left:
A slain Viking warrior by Gustav Vigeland

One gets the impression of Vigeland as a meticulous master, perfecting the human form and then contorting it to his will. An especially disturbing pair of sculptures by Vigeland show a skeletal form that was once a human being absorbed into a tree. A man looks on in horror from another tree, watching the scene unfold. Does he know he'll be next? Is it a metaphor for what will happen to us all?

HOW TO HAVE AN ADVENTURE IN SCANDINAVIA

Ultimately, Vigeland's profoundly nightmarish and sometimes outrageous art is unexplained in symbolism. The closest he got to an explanation was a single statement dedicated to the towering obelisk of swarming humans. He said of it, per the museum exhibit, "the column is my religion."

Frogner Park has a few cafes where you can sit and enjoy a drink, and maybe some food. I bought an iced tea and sat at a table in the shade, cooling off just meters away from the the surreal dreamworld I'd just experienced. It was a lovely afternoon, courtesy of a master of the bizarre.

Finished with my iced tea, it was time for dinner. That evening, I'd sample the other end of traditional Norwegian cuisine — seafood — in one of Oslo's best restaurants for it.

Lofotstua was just down the Kirkeveien from the park's main gate. Its entrance was unassuming, just another storefront on a major street with some tables in the window. Inside, traditional fishing-themed Norwegian decor greeted me along with the friendly owner.

A charming, old fashioned restaurant, Lofotstua specializes in fresh Norwegian fish caught in Norway's northern seas. Venison is great, but the true pride of Norway is seafood. Let me tell you, it lives up to the hype.

To begin, I ordered my second aquavit of the trip. I decided to try Simers Taffel — a bit sweeter and more straightforward than Opland, but just as delicious.

Lofotstua's owner (also my waiter) knew his stuff. He proved his expertise on the food his restaurant served, and introduced me to the menu as I poured over its options, all of which looked amazing.

"These fish are all caught in Denmark, right?" I blurted out, having briefly forgotten which country I was in.

His look of utter confusion snapped me to attention.

"Norway," I corrected myself with a laugh, "I mean Norway."

He very proudly explained to me that all of the restaurant's fish were indeed caught in Norway, particularly in the Arctic region at that time of year. The cold water makes the arctic the best place in Norway for fish.

HOW TO HAVE AN ADVENTURE IN SCANDINAVIA

This was a fantastic sign for my coming journey north, as I was going to an area legendary for having the best fish in all of Europe.

The Lofoten Islands were where the restaurant got its name. They're home to many respected fisheries, but lots of great fish are also caught in the further Troms region where my voyage would take me.

When I mentioned that I was headed up to Tromsø the next week, he told me of a special addition to the menu that he described as "the jewel of the North" dating back to the Middle Ages.

Bokna fisk is a Troms region delicacy, arctic caught cod served fermented as it would've been in the medieval era. He warned that it was richer than I might expect. I was on an adventure after all, so I informed him that I was up to the challenge.

Finished with my aquavit, I noticed that the restaurant carried a craft beer from the region of its name. Lofotpils is a Pilsner brewed on the Lofoten islands with all local ingredients except the hops, which are imported from Belgium as Norway is a bit beyond the range of the ideal hops-growing climate.

The Bokna fisk was, as expected, fantastic — truly the delicacy of the Medieval Nords.

Left:
Bokna Fisk at Lofotstua

RAFFAEL CORONELLI

The fermented cod's taste was intense and transportive, full of deep, rich flavor that comes from drying over the ocean; it can never touch land during that period. It tastes strongly of having come from beyond the north waves. I would recommend trying it while taking into consideration the level that you can handle very rich fish. It was more than alright for me.

I thanked the waiter afterwards, not just for introducing me to this traditional Norwegian dish, but also for his incredible depth of knowledge of Norwegian seafood. If you go to Lofotstua, ask him about the fish you're ordering. He'll tell you, and it will definitely be interesting.

Lofotstua was without a doubt my favorite restaurant in Oslo for its incredible food, excellent service, and charming atmosphere.

Full of delicious cured fish, I hopped on the tram back to the East End. It was an interesting experience riding what is essentially a train in the middle of the street, providing the view of a bus from tracks that rumble along a preordained path. I made it back to the hotel tired from the eventful day. The next would be a day of travel across Central Norway, through the mountains, to a very different part of the country.

Journey to Bergen:
Over the Realm of Giants

Somehow, somewhere on my walks through the West End the previous day, I'd pulled a ligament in my left knee. It wasn't debilitating, but it did make bending my knee somewhat painful and gave me a strange gait with my left leg not unlike Boris Karloff stumbling around as Frankenstein's Monster. The rest of the trip would be full of walking, so I decided that looking a little unusual was preferable to not being able to do any of the things I'd planned. That's life at 30!

I'd had a great time in Oslo, taking in unmissable sights and getting a crash-course in Norwegian culture. It'd been the perfect introduction to the rest of the trip.

I found myself having to follow the map to the train station less that time, having acclimated to Oslo's winding streets on this route. By that standard, I'd say it takes about three or four times going anywhere in Oslo to remember how to get there.

For breakfast while I bided my time, I ducked into another Kaffebrenneriet location by the station. As usual, I began ordering in Norwegian in what was probably a very silly American accent.

"Jeg vil ha en Tors Hammer," I ordered a "Thor's Hammer," a cup of black coffee with a shot of espresso.

"For here?" the barista answered in English.

"Yeah," I laughed. "It's the accent, isn't it?"

"It's just easier," he replied, "but it's good to try."

For breakfast, I got a Mueslibrød — bread filled with muesli, the German-originated mixed granola.

RAFFAEL CORONELLI

By 10:00, I was on the platform awaiting the arrival of the Bergensbanen.

The railway connecting Oslo Sentralstasjon to Bergen Station over a 6-hour ride, the Bergensbanen stretches across central Norway and is heralded by some as the most scenic railway in the world. I'm inclined to agree, though I haven't been on every railway.

Tickets must be booked before hand, especially if you want to sit in first class. I'm not usually one to splurge on those things, but first class on the Bergensbanen though Norway's Vy train operating service wasn't too much more than a regular ticket. The only must is to make sure you pick a window seat. It doesn't matter which side, though mine on the right side was excellent.

The Bergensbanen in Oslo Sentralstasjon

HOW TO HAVE AN ADVENTURE IN SCANDINAVIA

First class included a few perks. Notable among them was an automatic coffee machine that made various coffee-based drinks. Being in the first class cabin entitled me to use it for free. Such machines are not always free as they were here, as I found out the hard way a few days later.

Seated as the train pulled away from Oslo Sentralstasjon, I watched the city vanish behind us. I was embarking into the wilder, more primal parts of Norway — a realm of great, vast forests, towering mountains, and mythical creatures.

One such creature residing in central Norway was the Bøyg. Something similar to a troll, the Bøyg was an entity of sinister intelligence said to live in the mountains of Telemark and prevent the passage of travelers.

The title character in *Peer Gynt* had a run-in with the Bøyg during his romp through the Hall of the Mountain King, receiving a more considerable threat from its mystic power than from the trolls he'd met previously. The Bergensbanen grazes the north border of Telemark on its way across the country, bringing us into the Bøyg's mountainous territory. "Bøyg" itself means "twist," possibly referring to a serpent-like appearance, but also referencing the winding mountain paths one must traverse to pass through the region.

RAFFAEL CORONELLI

Not far out of Oslo, the train began following twists and turns around the ever-growing mountains. Not quite snow-capped yet, each one appeared taller than the last as we approached the mighty line of stone-and-ice giants that stand at Norway's center — Jotunheimen.

With every turn around a mountain lake, with every plunge into the dark of a tunnel bored into rock, the landscape grew in extremity. The train climbed in elevation 4,000 ft / 1,200 meters into the mountain range. (Its largest peak, further north, is twice that height). Soon snow covered the ground, and we were in the land of the jötunn.

HOW TO HAVE AN ADVENTURE IN SCANDINAVIA

Glacier in the Jotunheimen Mountains

Jotunheim, a realm in Norse myth from which the mountains get their name, is the land where the jötunn dwell. These giants are the root of Norway's troll folklore, and frequently had interactions with the gods — most notably Loki, fathered by a jötunn. Thor fought with jötunn on several occasions, the giants making formidable adversaries. The ancestor of all jötunn, Ymir, was part of the creation myth; his enormous body formed the foundations of the Earth.

Great glaciers stretched between the peaks, trees becoming scarcer with every increase in elevation. A giant would not have been out of place in the scene outside the window — and neither would an Imperial Walker.

RAFFAEL CORONELLI

Finse

The train reached its zenith in elevation at 4,009', at Finse station. Covered in snow, Finse is a ski resort, but holds another notable distinction.

Finse was a filming location for a little movie from 1980 of which you may have heard called *The Empire Strikes Back*. Looking for a place to represent the ice planet Hoth in outdoor location footage, George Lucas, Irvin Kirshner, and company chose Finse's Hardangerjøkulen glacier — perhaps unaware of the ordeal involved.

Getting the film crew to the location by train was the easy part; Finse's extreme weather, including a particularly harsh snow storm, caused unprecedented delays in filming. Harrison Ford, joining the crew after his scenes were moved from a studio shoot to the location, had to make part of the journey to the partly buried set in a snow plow. Norwegian rescue skiers on hand to help in case of emergency ended up acting as extras playing Rebel soldiers during the battle scene. The authenticity of the crew's braving the elements came across on screen as characters traversed the cold glacial expanse.

HOW TO HAVE AN ADVENTURE IN SCANDINAVIA

My view of Finse was much more comfortable. I didn't schedule any time to get off the train to have a look around. Unless you're on skis, there isn't much you can do there. Watching from inside was fine, and I had other outdoor experiences coming up.

RAFFAEL CORONELLI

Vestland

Snow turned to rain and mist as the train descended from the Jotunheimens into the Vestland region. Overcast skies shrouded the winding tracks and mountain lakes in low-hanging fog, creating an eerie atmosphere.

It was out of this foreboding scene that Bergen emerged drenched in columns of rain at the edge of a western fjord. Something about this city under a storm cloud was the atmosphere I'd imagined from this part of Norway — northern darkness, indeed.

As I'd previously mentioned, Bergen gets a lot of rain and is, in fact, the wettest city in all of Europe. This is because the Gulf Stream — the weather current that prevents Norway from having the climate of, say, Greenland — funnels precipitation across the Atlantic from the Caribbean. This precipitation hits Norway's lower west coast head-on, and a lot of it funnels right down Byfjorden to the city of Bergen that sits tucked into a valley at its end.

Knowing this before hand, I'd bought and packed a poncho for hiking around Bergen — a good idea if you want to stay dry and still experience the natural areas that rub right up against the city center.

HOW TO HAVE AN ADVENTURE IN SCANDINAVIA

What I'd forgotten to bring was something more convenient to use at short notice — an umbrella.

Luckily, downtown Bergen is much more compact and easier to navigate than Oslo. Right out of the train station, mountains loomed just beyond the city center. Fløyen was the peak I'd hike to the next day, aided by the Floibanen Funicular that goes partway up the mountainside from a convenient location.

My hotel, another less-than-glamorous establishment, was located inside the Xhibition shopping center. The check-in desk closed before my arrival, so I had to self-check-in at a locked key box on the ground floor like an AirBNB. The hotel room was fine, just enough to serve as a base camp for my time in the city's center area. Conveniently, anything I wanted to buy was available in the adjacent shopping mall, so I bought an umbrella to use on my walk to dinner.

Dinner was at Pingvinen, a pub and restaurant that serves traditional Bergen cuisine and an array of local beers. Seated by myself at the bar, a woman sat next to me and asked if the seat was taken in Norwegian.

"I'm not using it!" I replied in English.

It didn't take long to realize that she was an American expat — a professor of English literature at the University of Bergen, Laura Miles. As to be expected from a professor, she turned out to be a font of knowledge about numerous subjects — from Bergen, to Norwegian culture, to Medieval English interactions with the Nords. I can only imagine that her classes are extremely interesting, as would be the academic book she was planning to write.

Professor Miles had a meeting with fellow academics from the university at an adjacent restaurant. She left me the rest of the olives she'd ordered as a snack and gave me her business card so that I could include her while writing the book with proper attribution.

RAFFAEL CORONELLI

Plukkfisk at Pingvinen

Not wanting to just have olives for dinner, I ordered plukkfisk. A hearty Bergen classic, plukkfisk is a mashed up mixture of cod and potatoes. Bergen has been the site of fisheries for its entire existence. Bryggen, which I'd visit the next day, used to be a place where fishermen and traders could unload their items into warehouses. Today, large fish warehouses still dot the shore of the fjord where trawlers come in with their catches.

HOW TO HAVE AN ADVENTURE IN SCANDINAVIA

A couple of beers in, I decided to try asking the bar tender something related to the following day's plans.

"I'm going to Galleri Fjalar tomorrow," I told him. "Have you ever met Gaahl?"

"He comes in here quite a lot," said the bar tender.

Gaahl is local celebrity in Bergen, not only a painter and gallery owner but a legendary Black Metal vocalist whose music I'd listened to since I was a teenager. I was looking forward to seeing his paintings the next day at the gallery. The notion of meeting him in Bergen was something I'd considered unlikely, but entertained nonetheless.

Leaving that thought for the following afternoon when the gallery opened, I paid my tab and headed back to the hotel. My first order of business in Bergen would be my first hike in the Norwegian wilderness.

Bergen

Central Bergen:
At the Foot of the Humming Mountain

Central Bergen, as I observed on arrival, is compact and easily navigable — a far cry from the labyrinths of Oslo. Also striking is how it brushes right up against the mountains that serve as a barrier around the city.

The closest of these mountains was Fløyen, at the top of the Floibanen funicular. Grabbing a croissant, a coffee, and a bottle of water for the hike from a 7 Eleven (which was a little interesting to see the differences in a chain from one country to the next), I headed up Vetrildsallmenningen (quite the street name) to the Floibanen station.

The way attractions in central Bergen are so close together in such a scenic locale makes it feel a bit like a theme park land. The difference, of course, is that Bergen is real and everything you do will have absolute authenticity. The Floibanen station at the end of the the street does greet you a bit like the entrance to a ride.

The first ride was at 8:00 AM, so I arrived just before hand and bought a return ticket at one of the automatic kiosks by the entrance. Getting there as soon as it opened meant that I walked right in with no crowd whatsoever. The line would extend out the door just a few hours later, so I recommend Fløyen as a morning destination to get to as early as possible.

RAFFAEL CORONELLI

Floibanen ground-level station

One of three funicular railways in Norway, Floibanen operates with two carriages that counterbalance each other at opposite ends. One sat at the top, the station partway up the mountain. I found the other docked in the lower station's embarkation room, nearly empty, with open doors beside a staircase-shaped platform with each step leading to a different level of the carriage. Wanting the best view on the way up, I seated myself in the lowest row. The window gave a close-up view of a concrete wall, but I knew that would soon change.

The carriage rumbled gently and ascended through a long concrete tunnel. The walls fell away and Bergen spread out beneath, rocks and mountainside shrubs zooming past below the windows.

HOW TO HAVE AN ADVENTURE IN SCANDINAVIA

Bergen from the ascending Floibanen

In panoramic view from above, central Bergen looked even more like a fantasy town. Bryggen, where I'd spend my afternoon, waited by the waterfront. A medieval fortress, Bergenhus festning, lay just beyond it.

More shockingly, the entire city was bathed in sunlight. Just about every day in Bergen gets some precipitation, so I wasn't holding my breath, but the bright clarity aiding my view from the funicular's back window felt like tremendous luck. The old gods were smiling on me that day, and Thor had cleared the skies over Bergen.

Docked at the top, the doors opened and I exited through the station to a blast of mountain wind. A sheer drop from a platform with a short railing overlooked Bergen from the mountainside. This veranda was a fantastic vantage point, but also might be a little nerve-wracking if you have any issues with heights.

Having been on the first carriage up, I and the others who'd rode with me were the only ones there. This added to the void-like feeling of being next to such a precipice. I turned and followed the signs in the other direction to my reason for going up to Fløyen — the hiking trails into the mountain forest.

One of the signs read something particularly enticing — "Troll Forest". A *Troll Forest*, on a Norwegian mountain! For a first hike in the Nordic wilderness, this couldn't have been themed more perfectly. It was time to face down these forests' oldest residents.

Taking the path up a small hill, a wooden stump lay ahead. Approaching, its details came into focus and I saw what it was — the head of a troll. What remained of a decapitated troll had been left sticking out of the ground, possibly as a warning.

I kept walking, encountering a wooden post. Atop it was mounted the head of another troll. Soon the pikes multiplied like a battlefield visited by Vlad Dracula. Some of the wooden troll heads had their faces bashed in, while others were more intact but left without their bodies. It had been a massacre.

HOW TO HAVE AN ADVENTURE IN SCANDINAVIA

Remains of an unfortunate troll in the Troll Forest on Fløyen

The Troll Forest, an easy path decorated with carnage for the amusement of children, was an interesting first encounter on the mountain. I wouldn't be seeing any live trolls that day with the warm sun still bathing the area (trolls turn to stone in sunlight), so I had to be satisfied with this mildly horrific display. This would not be my most substantial encounter with Norway's troll mythology on the trip, but a more in-depth look would have to wait for another day, in another place.

Done with the troll graveyard, I continued deeper into the woods. My next stop would be the mountain's summit. To point my way there, I followed the sign marked with the mountain's name, Fløyen.

The path wound up into the forest, over vines and roots. The canopy grew denser, nature's embrace encompassing. Being out in nature can give you peace of mind in ways you can't explain, and the more vast the space, the stronger it feels. The Norwegian wilderness is nothing if not vast and immersive, even such a short distance from the city center of Bergen.

My knee still bothered me a bit, so I picked up a sizable fallen tree branch and used it like a wizard's staff. Eventually it grew heavy and I tossed it to the side of the trail, but at least I got to experience walking like a wizard in a Norwegian forest for a bit.

Up the steep hiking trail, I climbed over rocks and mountain streams that flowed downward across the path. A tiny waterfall trickled down from some overhanging rocks by the trail side. I wouldn't recommend drinking water that's been flowing over dirt, but it can be useful for other things — like washing the mud off of my hiking boots, and the dirt from my hands that accumulated while carrying the walking stick. The water's icy flow made me feel one with the mountain, its rejuvenating lifesblood streaming through my fingers. The sound of the tiny stream babbling over the rocks was meditative, clearing my thoughts to nothing but the present; transcendent serenity, as I'd experience a few times in the wilds of the trip.

Fløyen extends 400 meters (1,300 feet) above the shoreline below, which isn't terribly high by mountain standards. Still, I don't think I'd ever climbed to the top of a mountain before in my life.

I'm not a mountain climber. I don't own a pickaxe or climbing gear — but you don't need one to reach the top of Fløyen. That doesn't mean you shouldn't be careful.

HOW TO HAVE AN ADVENTURE IN SCANDINAVIA

The path grew steeper and more rugged, dirt turning to boulders over which I had to climb. Up it pointed — to the summit.

In Norse mythology, mountains are made from the bones of the giant Ymir — the ancestor of all giants and trolls, whose carcass was used by the gods to form the foundations of the Earth. Nearing the peak, I dug my boots into notches in these bones of the Earth-sized giant as they protruded from the dirt, imperfections in the surface preventing me from sliding off and plummeting 400 meters.

Rocky path to the summit of Fløyen

RAFFAEL CORONELLI

Fløyen's summit

Drawing myself up onto the last boulder, I noticed a concrete pillar at its highest point. This marker let me know where I was — at the summit of Fløyen.

Stepping up to the pillar, I grasped it and dug my boots into the rock beneath. I'm not debilitatingly afraid of heights, but I do get somewhat uneasy in situations where I could easily fall. This felt like a moment of conquest over any such sensation, while still being extremely careful not to fall to my death. Even my pulled knee ligament wasn't an issue as I stood fast in the icy wind.

From that vantage point, I could see Bergen far below, and the waters of Byfjorden beyond. This was the view of the old gods when they looked down on their realm. In that place, at that moment, as the cold wind blew across the pinnacle rock atop which I stood, I was amongst the pantheon.

HOW TO HAVE AN ADVENTURE IN SCANDINAVIA

Bergen from the summit of Fløyen

I felt a snowflake on my face. A small cloud drifted overhead, the first I'd seen that bright day. The top of Fløyen is high enough in altitude that rain becomes snow. Hardly any day in Bergen is without some precipitation, even a mostly sunny one, so it was fitting that the daily sprinkle happened while I was at the peak of the mountain. It was as if the old gods were giving me a greeting, sending a small sign from the weather to congratulate my ascent to the mountaintop. I couldn't help but smile at the thought.

It could have been Freyr's doing, an important Norse god who doesn't have quite as much of a pop culture presence as Thor but was just as important to the old Norse. Freyr is the god of summer and rain, and brings prosperity to crops. May is not quite summer in Norway, but it wouldn't be out of the question on such a nice day for him to have influence.

Skadi, goddess of winter and snow, could also have been the one who sent me this summit greeting of dancing snowflakes. Winter had made way for spring in Bergen, but she could've decided to service the mountaintop from her arctic summer retreat.

RAFFAEL CORONELLI

The author of this book trying not to fall off the summit of Fløyen

As much as I wanted to stay, I'd savored the moment and had to move on if I was going to do other things that day. After snapping a few photos while being careful not to become a person who falls off a mountain taking a timed selfie, I climbed down the boulder and descended the path.

Just below the summit, the snow defrosted into a drizzle of rain and provided me with an excuse to wear the poncho I'd bought for such an eventuality. Putting it on and transforming into some type of cloaked forest gnome, I stood amidst the brief gloom and once again enjoyed this greeting from the gods.

Right:
The author this book
in the rain on Fløyen

HOW TO HAVE AN ADVENTURE IN SCANDINAVIA

A path branched off from the one I was on, marked with the name Rundemansveien. This trail will take you all the way around several mountains in the area. I decided to follow it for a little while and then turn back. Hopping over babbling brooks and stumbling across boulders, I got to see more of the rolling mountainside terrain before heading back to the Floibanen station.

Almost to the station, I happened upon some mountain goats. Goats make their homes on mountains in Norway and are a staple of local wildlife.

These didn't seem to mind me while they munched on hay, though I also didn't want them to gore me with their horns, so I kept a safe distance. Goats are not eaten often in Norwegian cuisine the way venison is, probably because goats are scrawny and small, and not known for being especially tasty. A wolf might enjoy them, but a person would rather eat other things. Their presence on the mountain was a nice surprise meeting.

Back at the station, a crowd had amassed on the overlook platform in the time I'd been hiking. A goat was also there, seemingly accustomed to the tourists as it munched on grass on the hillside. Even with a return ticket, a seat was not guaranteed on the next funicular carriage unless I waited in line at the station. Within the half hour, I was seated on the funicular and on my way down from the mountaintop where I'd had such a transcendental experience.

RAFFAEL CORONELLI

Hiking had worked up my appetite, and there was one place near the funicular station that I absolutely had to try — a Bergen classic that those without dietary restrictions should give absolutely a shot.

Trekroneren (literally "the three coins") is a storefront sausage stand, a fast food staple that sells various authentic sausages for you to eat standing up. Their classic menu item that was my reason for seeking it out was distinctively Norwegian — a sausage made from reindeer meat.

I followed recommendations I'd heard and ordered a reindeer sausage with lingonberry jam. It doesn't get any more Norwegian than that! Standing by the roadside to eat my lunch, a pretty sizable sausage, I was struck by the dark, full flavor. The lingonberries complemented it perfectly, combining to form the authentic taste of the wild north.

Reindeer are herded on reindeer farms in northern Norway, so the reindeer you eat won't exactly be made from wild hunted animals. The Sami have been herding reindeer for most of their history, originating reindeer-based dishes that are especially popular in the arctic regions. This Norwegian reindeer sausage served with the country's signature berry was something I wouldn't be able to have anywhere else.

Right:
Reindeer sausage
at Trekroneren

HOW TO HAVE AN ADVENTURE IN SCANDINAVIA

Trekroneren

RAFFAEL CORONELLI

Bryggen

With lunsj taken care of, I headed onto the peninsula extending into the fjord. Colorful, uniform wooden buildings with triangular roofs lined up on the oceanfront — the Bryggen. These buildings house shops, art galleries, and restaurants today, but originally were warehouses built to offload cargo and fish from incoming traders who would pull right up to them. Cranes could extend from the top of the buildings to lift cargo off of boats and into the storage spaces. I'd explore this quaint neighborhood, a world heritage site, after I'd taken in the introduction at the Bryggens Museum.

The museum is located just after the end of the Bryggen buildings, before you get to Bergenhus fortress. It contains an in-depth exhibit showcasing an excavation of medieval artifacts from that very spot beneath the current Bryggen.

Due to a fire, most of the standing Bryggen buildings were built in the 18th Century. The original warehouses had stood on the site since at least the 14th Century.

HOW TO HAVE AN ADVENTURE IN SCANDINAVIA

The excavation in the Bryggens Museum is from the murky period of a few centuries after the end of the Viking Age, but before the arrival of international political influence on Norway from Denmark. The old Norse culture had evolved, and Bergen became a center of trade. Stockfish from the north and grain imports from mainland Europe to the south sat in the Bryggen's warehouses as a temporary home before being traded elsewhere.

One element of Viking culture that did not go by the wayside was their advanced shipbuilding style. Ships excavated near the Bryggen from this medieval time period were built using the same techniques the Vikings used centuries prior, with streamlined hulls and curved bows. With the efficiency of an ocean-crossing longship, they carried wares into the Bryggen and out of Byfjorden. Elsewhere in Norway, like the Lofoten Islands where delicious arctic fish are caught, shipbuilders continued to use Viking techniques into the 1940s — simply because they worked so well and didn't require changing. Much of modern archeologists' understanding of Viking ships is informed and complemented by the passing down of knowledge between generations of Norwegian shipbuilders. The museum's collection contains remains of a trading ship that showcases this.

Also on display are garments and personal affects of medieval residents, items that show what their way of life in medieval Bergen might have been like. Each display is a window to someone's existence centuries ago. The museum gives an appreciation for the Bryggen's history, and complemented my walk through it later on.

After the museum, I turned to the looming presence just further down the peninsula. Contrasting with the colorful wooden Bryggen, a grey castle stood as a sentry facing the sea.

RAFFAEL CORONELLI

Bergenhus Festning was not quite as immersive or expansive as Akershus, the previous festning I'd visited on the trip. This is simply because it's not very big, hasn't been in many battles, and doesn't take a lot of time to see — which is actually fine, since you'll want to spend more time in Bryggen just down the road, anyway.

Bergenhus is associated with one prominent historic battle — one which took place at sea, where the belligerent forces of two foreign countries fought in a neutral port. In August of 1665, the Dutch merchant and treasure fleet sailed into Bergen to deliver goods for trade at a port not controlled by their enemies, the English. The English, however, contested control of the trade route. Upon hearing of the Dutch fleet's avoidance of English-controlled waters to bring their expensive wares to Bergen, a fleet of English warships launched in pursuit. The resulting conflict in the waters of Byfjorden was the Battle of Vågen.

Norway was neutral, but King Frederick III of Denmark — to whom Norway answered — sought an alliance with England. To stop the battle from going in an unfavorable direction, the Danish king sent a frantic message northward urging the Norwegians at Bergenhus Fortress to side with the English. The order took too long to reach the city, and instead, the Norwegians helped the Dutch merchant fleet fight off the English warships.

The damage was done; a potential alliance with England was in shambles, even with a personal apology from Norwegian commander Claus von Ahlefeldt. Meanwhile, the Dutch enjoyed offloading their merchandise in freshly won safety, a boon to Bergen's trade economy.

I don't know about you, but I find this story hilarious. The punchline is the Norwegian commander having to apologize to Lord Sandwich for deciding to bombard the fleet who were objectively being the bigger jerks — and yes,

HOW TO HAVE AN ADVENTURE IN SCANDINAVIA

the English fleet was commanded by a man whose title was Lord Sandwich.

Cannon positions from which the Norwegians participated in the battle are located on the ramparts, which take a just a few minutes to walk around. The main attraction at Bergenhus is the Rosencrantz Tower.

Admission to the tower is required, but worth it. The basement allows you to see chambers that were once open to the ocean, where boats could sail right in to the fortress' lower level. Through the tower were exhibits on the goings on in the fortress through the centuries. Emerging onto the roof, I was treated to a 360-degree view of Bryggen on one side and Byfjorden on the other.

In 1531, Lord Bille of Bergenhus Castle became the first person to mention the drink aquavit by name in the historical record. It's unknown from where he got it (probably Denmark), but it's still a notable attribute for the fortress' reputation.

Having taken in the fortress, I headed back up the peninsula to wander through the alleyways of Bryggen.

Left:
Rosencrantz Tower
at Bergenhus Fortress

RAFFAEL CORONELLI

An alley in Bryggen

HOW TO HAVE AN ADVENTURE IN SCANDINAVIA

Putting aside its history, the most immediately noticeable thing about Bryggen is its uniformity of architecture. Each building is roughly the same size, shape, and material, painted in a different single shade. Most are warmer colors, either blood red or yellow-orange, with some white or a natural brown.

I wandered through its maze-like alleys, warm colors and nearly-enclosed spaces providing a cozy sensation. Bryggen is home to shops and a number of art galleries, some selling typical tourist wares, while others display unique pieces made by local artisans.

I enjoyed taking my time in a leisurely early afternoon browsing through the ones at ground level. Locals and tourists alike took in the inviting district that covers deceptively little space but with countless nooks and crannies hiding treasures for visitors to discover.

There was one space in particular that was my focused destination for the afternoon when it opened at 3:00PM. I'd visited places related to my interest in a certain notable Norwegian music genre already, but this was different. It was almost time to enter the wyrd world of a Bergen legend.

On the second floor of Bryggen 37, the last building on the second to last block on the waterfront, is Galleri Fjalar. The art gallery is owned by a singular figure in Bergen's contemporary culture — Kristian "Gaahl" Espedal, vocalist of bands like Trelldom, Gorgoroth, and currently the excellent Gaahls Wyrd. He's also known to some for his iconoclastic interviews and the impression that he's some kind of Vincent Price character who's somehow emerged into reality. That's the image and reputation, of course. The man behind it is a multifaceted artist of music, performance, and painting — the latter having influenced him to open his now world-famous gallery in Bryggen.

RAFFAEL CORONELLI

To be honest, I wasn't sure if he'd be there. Gaahl is a busy guy with his band and whatnot, and his partner seems to handle at least some of the gallery's management duties. My realistic goal was to see his deeply surreal artwork, along with the current guest exhibition which rotates regularly and features other interesting Norwegian artists of his selection. If I got to say a brief "hi" to someone whose work I'd admired and enjoyed for the better part of a couple decades, that would be a fantastic perk.

A small sign in the second story window displayed the gallery's name along with its Norse rune logo. Next to it on the corner of the building was a wooden carving of a man holding an axe, an original piece of the architecture that nonetheless contributed to the atmosphere. Another sign helpfully pointed the way up the stairs, directing foot traffic to the gallery.

The steps creaked one at a time as I ascended. What untamed forces I'd find remained hidden in shadow. At the top of the stairs, a tall figure came into view — a carved giant, a wood statue of an elongated man that stretched nearly to the ceiling. This visually arresting sculpture is the work of a local Bergen artist, Jan Henning Larsen. It was an imposing sight, and set the tone for the gallery perfectly.

Left:
Exterior of
Galleri Fjalar

HOW TO HAVE AN ADVENTURE IN SCANDINAVIA

Gaahl's paintings and a sculpture by Jan Henning Larsen
at the entrance to Galleri Fjalar

RAFFAEL CORONELLI

Then I turned to the gallery's door. From it, without pomp or circumstance, emerged a slender man in all black and a leather jacket with long brown hair drawn back in a ponytail, sporting a distinctive beard accentuating his sharp features. He was still setting up the just-opened gallery, moving paintings to display stands near the statue.

My eyes widened. One thought took hold of my mind.

It's Gaahl.

Between stage performances, album photos, and film clips I'd seen over the years, I could practically feel the zap between neurons connecting the dots telling me it was him.

"Hi!" I blurted. "It's great to meet you! I've been listening to your music for years! I came to see your artwork, but I didn't know you'd be here!"

I'm assuming the words came out with some semblance of intelligibility, because he smiled in return. If nothing else, my falling over myself at recognizing him must have been amusing.

"Thank you!" laughed Gaahl in his deep, lightly accented voice, "I'm usually here when I'm not, you know, on tour."

My first impressions of the real Gaahl — sans any theatrical elements — were disarming, immediately friendly, and happy to welcome visitors to his artistic lair. He explained with enthusiasm that the art on display inside the gallery was that of the guest artist on exhibition, but that his own paintings were the ones he'd just placed in the twin racks next to the sculpture. Each was in a plastic covering on a board, and he invited me to flip through.

"You can pick them up to get a better look!" he encouraged me.

Letting him finish opening the gallery, I flipped through the visual pieces from his artistic oeuvre. All of them had a distinct flavor of surrealism, bordering on expressionist.

HOW TO HAVE AN ADVENTURE IN SCANDINAVIA

Gaahl's art evokes a similar combination of dark topics painted with vivid, dreamlike palettes to Norway's own Edvard Munch. That said, his style is wholly unique and immediately distinctive.

It's remarkable to look at an artist who creates across different mediums and see correlations in their work; there's not too much of a thematic jump to see that both Gaahls Wyrd's *Gastir — Ghosts Invited* album and the surreal works before me were created with input by the same creative mind. I'd get a chance to ask Gaahl more about specific pieces a bit later.

Stepping into the interior space of Galleri Fjalar, a bright, inviting room covered in black and white art greeted me. A woman quietly browsed the drawings, the only other guest at that point.

The then-current artist on exhibit was Kim Diaz Holm, whose installation had just debuted the previous night. An entire wall displayed Holm's daily ink drawings of dark fantasy monsters that he creates in minutes. Each had a fun look and a unique design, all of which I appreciated as something of a monster connoisseur. Another wall showed Holm's self-portraits, fulfilling the "monster og meg" or "monster and me" theme.

Left:
Ink Monsters
by Kim Diaz Holm
in Galleri Fjalar
May 2022

121

"I'm going to have a coffee," Gaahl stated as he headed into the back room. "Do you want one?"

"Sure!" I blurted out as I heard the coffee machine rumble to life like a distant baseline buried in a hyper-distorted guitar mix.

Ok, Gaahl! I'll have a coffee! The guy I had on my MySpace when I was fifteen years old was making me a coffee. Life can put you in bizarre scenarios.

Gaahl emerged from the back with two coffees for the woman and I, already more hospitality than I'd ever expected. The coffee was as black as one could want from the dark master.

With continued enthusiasm, our host explained the newly opened exhibition. It'll have been replaced by another by the time you read this, but the standard it set is a good sign for things to come.

Kim Diaz Holm is a fellow Bergen-based artist who inhabits a whimsical fantasy realm with his creature designs, using a visceral art style that deals in clear forms and aggressive brushstrokes. I hadn't put it together yet, but he had done one prominent piece with which I was already familiar.

"Has he done any album covers?" I asked. "He seems like he'd be good at it."

"He did Abbath's *Outstrider* album," Gaahl mentioned.

That's where I'd seen his stuff, then! Olve "Abbath" Eikemo is a Bergen native who, like Gaahl, has evolved from his pioneering days in the early Norwegian Black Metal scene and continues to make great music. His eponymous band Abbath's 2019 album *Outstrider* featured cover art by Holm depicting his visage made out of tree branches and other pieces of the Norwegian wilderness.

HOW TO HAVE AN ADVENTURE IN SCANDINAVIA

Upon realizing I was a fan, Gaahl went to retrieve Holm's original drawings for the cover, which were on hand in the gallery. Seeing the forest of detail in the original drawing and concept sketches in person was incredible.

Also making the genre connection were Holm's musician portraits depicting a variety of artists, which Gaahl brought out. I knew I wanted to buy something from Gallery Fjalar, and these musician drawings were the perfect way to commemorate my visit. Of course, what better musician to buy in art form than the host himself? The piece I chose was a striking profile of Gaahl holding out a microphone onstage, an evocative and iconic image of the gallery owner's other artistic medium.

"He's very good at what he does," Gaahl remarked at my choice, a modest reaction to my clearly deciding to buy a picture someone drew of him looking cool.

The issue with buying art on a long trip is that it has to go home with you. Well aware of this, Gaahl crafted a sturdy piece of cardboard packaging that would keep it structurally sound in my bag as I continued through Scandinavia and then back to the US. It held up perfectly, and the piece now resides in a frame in my collection.

While he worked on creating the package, I flipped through a book of his own paintings. One in particular jumped out at me — a pair of men, both drawn in the elongated style typical of humans in Gaahl's paintings, but both in far different poses. One man held a severed head in one hand and knife in the other. The other man sat in a contemplative pose next to him, staring off into space.

"I'm interested in the relationship between these two figures," I said. "This guy's just decapitated somebody, but is this other guy thinking about it or ignoring it?"

"I painted that years ago," he laughed. "I don't remember what I was thinking, but I think ignoring it."

It seemed that he wanted to keep his art open to interpretation, an approach I respect. That insight into the character's motivation was a fascinating glimpse into the process behind such an eye-catching piece and its possible meanings.

Galleri Fjalar also sells T-shirts, which are printed just upstairs from the gallery. Gaahl informed me that they run big, so he recommended getting a size down from what I normally wear in US sizes.

"Are you sure?" I asked. "I've noticed that my band shirts from when I was a teenager don't fit me anymore these days."

He explained that the shirt sizes have only gotten bigger. Norwegians tend to be tall, and clothing sizes already run different in various countries. I took the recommendation and, sure enough, it ended up being the perfect fit.

Gaahl's long-term romantic partner is a male model, and he himself has been involved with the fashion world in various capacities. If he gives you advice on what to wear, you'd better listen.

Asked where else I was going on the trip, I said that my next stop would be Balestrand, about midway up the Sognefjord. (Gaahl ended up being the first person I ever heard give the correct pronunciation of "Balestrand" out loud, which sounds something like "Balessand.") We talked briefly about how he is originally from a town near the mouth of the Sognefjord, and goes back regularly to a place he has there — by boat, as he explained, which was to be my mode of transit to Balestrand the following day. He mostly lives in Bergen now, prompting him to joke about how long it would take if he had to go all the way back there from the gallery every day.

"It's the biggest fjord in Norway," I said, "right?"

"Oh, yeah," he replied, "It's kind of insane."

HOW TO HAVE AN ADVENTURE IN SCANDINAVIA

Gaahl with the author of this book in Galleri Fjalar

Before leaving, I asked Gaahl for a photo, to which he obliged. As I pulled up my phone camera, he straightened his posture and put on a more composed face. His eyes pierced into the lens, a severity I recognized. The photo taken, he went back to his disarming self.

"This has been fantastic," I said, "A real highlight of my trip. It's always great when you meet people whose work you respect, and they turn out to be really cool."

"Well," he laughed, "hopefully we are just normal people."

At no point was it lost on me that one of the most enjoyable and fun conversations I had on the entire trip was with none other than the "Destroyer" himself. Beyond all of that, he was just a cool guy to talk with who runs a great art gallery — a must-visit in Bryggen.

RAFFAEL CORONELLI

In 2023, he informed me, the gallery would double its size and devour even more of the second floor of the building. If you make it to the gallery after that happens, there should be twice as much art to take in.

When it came time to pay for my purchases, he had me take a look at the computer.

"I think this is right," he said. "I'm bad at math."

Self-deprecating humor is all the funnier coming from a guy with such a reputation. With a handshake and a farewell, I left Galleri Fjalar with an art piece, a shirt, and an unbeatable memory of a wonderfully human encounter.

What a day it had been. I'd looked down on Bergen from the summit of Fløyen. I'd tried reindeer sausage for lunch. I'd seen a medieval fortress and walked the colorful alleyways of a world heritage neighborhood. I'd met Gaahl!

Back in the room that evening, I took out my iPad, plugged in my headphones, and put on *The Humming Mountain* EP by Gaahls Wyrd — mesmerizing as ever.

Gaahl drawn by Kim Diaz Holm
art from Galleri Fjalar in the author's collection

Roaming Bergen:
Before the Voyage

My last stop between a quick doner kabob (Norway's favorite imported fast food) dinner at Norwegian chain Yummy Time and heading up to bed had been a REMA 1000, a convenience and grocery chain that sells essentials. I grabbed the largest bottle of water I could find for my upcoming hikes in Balestrand. I'd need it.

The thing about having a boat to catch at 4:00PM is that once you check out of your hotel, you have to lug all your belongings with you for the whole day. Not to complain — I wasn't going to let that or my still-sprained knee ligament stop me from enjoying the better part of another day in Bergen's city center.

My adventures in Bergen up to that point had been nothing if not action-packed, but there were still some nearby spots I hadn't seen. This day would be a more relaxed one to wander Bergen and enjoy the city until the boat left from the NORLED dock. Fortunately for me, it was another rare bright and clear day in Bergen.

Having used the automatic checkout and never interacted with a single hotel clerk in my stay, I walked a couple blocks southwest to one of the most scenic open inland spaces in the city — the combo of the green Julemarked Byparken on the northwest, and the paved Festplassen plaza stretching to the southeast.

Byparken has a gazebo in its center that is sometimes used for musical performances. Festplassen surrounds a small lake, Lille Lungegårdsvannet, which has a fountain at its center. This idyllic park was where I sat and applied sunscreen. Needing sunscreen in Bergen is like needing an umbrella in Death Valley, but again, I wasn't complaining.

RAFFAEL CORONELLI

Festplassen with Fløyen in the background

Beyond the fountain, Fløyen loomed over the city. The Floibanen station hung on the mountainside, above it the area where I'd taken my hike the previous morning — trolls and all, though those were hidden in the trees. Sunlight shimmered on the lake. It was a peaceful start to a day with no rain forecast.

Just past the southeast corner of Festplassen lay a hulking brown building — Grieghallen, or literally "The Grieg Hall". It's one of the biggest buildings in central Bergen and stands as a monument of sorts to one of the city's most famous sons, though it was built in the mid 20th Century, long after his death.

Edvard Grieg, one of the major artists of the 19th Century's Romantic period, was foundational for modern Norwegian culture. The romanticism of his symphonic works drew directly from Norse folklore and folk music.

HOW TO HAVE AN ADVENTURE IN SCANDINAVIA

I'd have a more substantial encounter with Grieg's legacy at a more personal and informative location in a couple of days, but I did enjoy wandering around the outside thinking about the countless recordings that took place on the premises. A century after Grieg, Bergen's Black Metal acts would follow in his wake. Several landmark albums were recorded in the hall's recording studio. Even my recent acquaintance Gaahl recorded two albums there with his first band Trelldom.

For breakfast, I went to Godt Brød, a bakery and coffee shop chain that originated in Bergen and now has locations in several Norwegian cities. While the nation to the south is enthusiastic enough about baking that an entire pastry subcategory is named after it in the English-speaking world (more on "danishes" much later in the book), Norwegians are not averse to pastries themselves. I ordered a cappuccino and a sommerbolle, "summer bun".

Sommerboller are decadent Norwegian pastries of various sizes, but one defined shape — a circular swirl of lightly frosted bread around an egg custard filling at the center. The one I got was fairly large. Sinking my teeth into the pastry's outer part, it reminded me of a soft cinnamon bun. The yellow custard at the center was creamy and sweet. In another country without proper background on what it is, I could imagine someone mistakenly calling it a "danish".

RAFFAEL CORONELLI

The Hordagut docked in Bergen

Post-pastry, I went for a walk by the waterfront by Bryggen. A light sea breeze rolled in off the fjord.

A gargantuan metal ship sat docked next to Bergenhus fortress, the *Hordagut*. This was a fishing trawler, bringing in the catch to Bergen's fish warehouses just like medieval fisherman had done at Bryggen in times long past. Some things don't change — only the technology. Cranes and other devices adorned the back of the massive vessel, a sturdy hulk that one could imagine weathering even the strongest ocean storm. Upon researching the vessel, I found that it operates at the time of this writing in the area around the Sognefjord, where I'd be later that day.

Continuing the theme, I continued around the tip of the peninsula to a row of massive modern warehouses. This modern-day equivalent to Bryggen's now-quaint wooden buildings are where fish are offloaded and prepared. The fish industry is still a big part of the local economy, and these buildings are where North Sea and fjord-caught seafood goes to the marketplace.

Walking down the other side of the peninsula, I faced Skutevik Bay. This less-visited inlet is no less scenic than the Bryggen side, but far less crowded with visitors. Colorful wooden buildings like those in Bryggen lined the shore, but these were still in use for their original utilitarian purpose.

HOW TO HAVE AN ADVENTURE IN SCANDINAVIA

Skutevik

I came across a small park wedged between two buildings overlooking the water. I sat on a concrete bench, if only to put down my bag for a little while, and gazed out at the bay. I was in no hurry and had no schedule until the late afternoon. It was a serene morning made more so by my being the only person at that spot.

Boats came and went. The sun blazed in the cloudless sky. Byfjorden beckoned me to begin my voyage north, but I still had a few hours to kill.

Having enjoyed my respite, I packed up and headed back up the peninsula, making a brief stop on the "Famous Wharf Skuteviksbrygge" — a small wood-planked wharf that sticks out into the bay. A small dog ran up to me with a short tree branch, wanting me to throw it for him to fetch. Its owner, a young woman, ran over and apologized to me. We both laughed, after which she threw the stick into the water, prompting the dog jumped in after it. He was a good swimmer, and quickly returned with the stick.

RAFFAEL CORONELLI

Past Bergenhus, I found myself back at Bryggen. I decided to grab a cup of coffee for something to do. Baker Brun is across the alley from Galleri Fjalar, and has an outdoor seating area where I was able to sit in the sun and enjoy my drink in view of Bergenhus Fortress, the harbor, and Bryggen 37, where I'd had such a memorable time the previous afternoon.

A modern warship rolled into the harbor with Norwegian navy officers standing on deck to greet the city. I watched it pass while sipping my coffee.

It was the Hitra, a Norwegian submarine chaser from World War II when it operated out of Scotland on missions for the exiled Royal Norwegian Navy to combat German U-boats. Still in use by the Norwegian Navy for ceremonial purposes, it lies anchored in the Bergen harbor when not touring the coastline.

The Hitra docked in Bergen

HOW TO HAVE AN ADVENTURE IN SCANDINAVIA

It was now afternoon. That sommerbolle wasn't getting me through the rest of the day until my arrival in Balestrand, so I headed back up the street to Trekroneren. I'd already had the must-try reindeer sausage with lingonberries, so I perused the rest of their extensive menu. I ended up getting a "wild game" jagdwurst with an herb sauce. It was a good second choice, the herbs complementing the taste.

Still a couple hours to go, I decided there was one thing left to do. It was beer o'clock. Jutting out of the end of the bay between Bryggen and the NORLED terminal was a pier on which there are, without exaggeration, about six or seven bars. They're all fairly similar tourist trap sports bars, but they all have an excellent view of the harbor and serve beverages, so you can't really go wrong if you're stuck there waiting for a boat like I was.

Thus, I wandered into one of them on the second floor of the bar complex. A bar tender cleaned glasses while waiting for patrons, so I walked right up.

"Do you have Aass?" I asked.

I'd had excellent craft beers on Norway, but I wanted to at least try the low-end generic stuff.

"Aass," he said in recollection, "the Norwegian beer! Sorry, we don't. We have Hansa, that's from Bergen!"

Indeed, Hansa is one of Norway's mass-produced beers and is made in Bergen. Locals take pride in it, rare for a non-craft Norwegian beer.

"Do you know Ringnes?" he asked. "That beer's from Oslo. We have a saying in Bergen about drinking Hansa and pissing Ringnes."

I laughed at what was clearly a jab at Oslo. I found this inter-city rivalry most amusing, especially relating to something like mass-produced beer. The bar tender was a nice guy, and seemed like a down-to-earth Bergen native. I'd imagine he's a fan of Bergen's football team, into which I'm sure the inter-city beer rivalry plays.

RAFFAEL CORONELLI

Hansa is a fine, smooth Pilsner — nothing more, nothing less. Sometimes that's all you need.

"Try the bar downstairs," he said as I finished, "the Flying Dutchman. They have more beer options."

I thanked him and headed downstairs for beer number 2. Walking up to the bar, I again asked for an Aass. I was determined to try it, just because I thought the name was funny. The bar tender at this one had no idea what I was talking about. She was clearly less knowledgeable about Norwegian beer than the guy upstairs, and had no amusing anecdotes making fun of Oslo. I did, however, order a Kjuagutt — a pretty good amber ale also made in Bergen. The Flying Dutchman had a nice patio where one could sit and look out at the harbor. I sipped my øl and watched the waves, biding my time until I could go out on them.

The NORLED terminal was directly across the harbor from Bryggen. The ticket office was closed and had no one staffing it, to the dismay of some tourists. I'd bought my ticket to Balestrand months before, which is highly recommended.

You can't go north from Bergen except by boat or plane. This is because the fjords cut into the coastline to such a degree that a train line is impossible. One could conceivably drive to Balestrand, but you'd have to go all the way around the Sognefjord or put your car on a ferry — at which point you're taking a boat anyway, so you may as well skip renting a car and do as the Vikings did.

The ship moored at the terminal was the *Tyrving*, a pontoon "express boat" that carries passengers between Bergen and towns on the Sognefjord. A topside deck allowed for observation, but most of the seats were in a sizable enclosed cabin below. This would be a necessity, as the elements on the fjord would be a lot to handle on deck — even on a day with such perfect weather.

HOW TO HAVE AN ADVENTURE IN SCANDINAVIA

The Tyrving docked in Bergen prior to departure

Metal clanked underfoot as I stepped aboard, the friendly captain checking my ticket. The spacious cabin had plenty of seats available. I chose one on the port side (left facing frontward), my window overlooking the waterfront Bryggen buildings across the harbor.

Other passengers filed in. Two women speaking German sat down in the row behind me. The guy in front of me turned around and asked in Norwegian-accented English if he could lay his seat back, an action I approved. It was nice of him to ask.

The engine rumbled. The boat rocked in the churned-up waves and pulled away from the shore. Slowly, it rotated 180 degrees until Bryggen was on the opposite side. I took that as my cue to head topside and see the city off.

Climbing the stairway to the deck hatch, I emerged into bright sunlight and a cool breeze. I moved to the railing at the back of the boat in time to see Bryggen pass — the boat moving by Galleri Fjalar, which would've been open at the time. Bergenhus fortress was next, its stone edifice announcing that we'd passed the barrier to Bergen's harbor.

Leaving Bergen on the Tyrving

The fish warehouses and massive trawlers docked by them saw us off. Beyond Skutevik Bay, I could see the wharf and the small seaside bench where I'd sat that morning. The Norwegian maritime flag on the back of the boat flapped in the wind. The *Tyrving* had left the back of Byfjorden and was now moving outward to the sea. The voyage had begun.

The Sognefjord:
Into the North Waves

Wind blew harder now that the ship was out on the waters of Byfjorden, prompting me to return to my seat and take in the views from the window. Situated comfortably in my own row, I watched Byfjorden roll by.

Not the biggest or most majestic fjord, Byfjorden still has that western Norway ruggedness once you get out of the city. Towns clung to the slopes of hills that jutted up out of the sea, outposts of humanity in the Nordic wilds.

The boat turned and we slipped out of Byfjorden and through the inter-fjord passages that would take us due north. Weaving between the islands separated from the mainland by tiny straights, the *Tyrving* navigated the complex western waterways.

Enclosed in the main cabin, I watched large panel windows assailed by seawater spraying up from churning waves as the vessel weaved through rocky passages.

Getting up to see what refreshments were available, I was pleasantly surprised to see a coffee machine identical to the one in first class on the Bergensbanen. Thinking it was freely available for use like that one was (it wasn't), I went to get a drink. An "out of order" sign mercifully put off my embarrassing mistake for two days.

Back at my seat, I watched as we moved through the small channel and onto open water between two shoreline rows of medium-sized mountains comparable to Fløyen. It wasn't the Sognefjord, but a smaller fjord to the south of it — Fensfjorden. Scenic in its own right, the Fensfjord dwarfed the *Tyrving* as it traversed the space between its southern and northern shores. This was but an appetizer for what was to come.

RAFFAEL CORONELLI

Moving back into the inter-fjord straights, rocky crags moved past the boat. I decided to climb topside again to get a better view. Just as I exited, I saw something big in the distance, obscured by hills and islands between. There was still a ways to go, but I could sense that we were getting closer to one of Norway's great vistas. I returned below deck, knowing I'd go back up when the time came.

One last smaller fjord lay in the *Tyrving*'s path — the Gulafjord. In itself, its tree-lined hillsides on either side of a winding straight were scenic enough without comparison. Still, something loomed out the front window, beyond the Gulafjord's northern side.

I had to go back topside. Climbing the steps and opening the deck hatch, I turned to the front bow in time to see the inter-fjord passage open at the end. On the other side were snow-capped peaks rising from the churning waves. My breath left me.

The *Tyrving* turned starboard as it exited the channel. I held fast to the port-side railing and stared out the shores of a series of islands to the north of the Sognefjord's mouth.

The Tyrving enters the Sognefjord

HOW TO HAVE AN ADVENTURE IN SCANDINAVIA

The Sognefjord

Past the island of Losna was the mainland mountain range that formed the north rim of the Sognefjord. Into it slipped the boat, and Norway's largest fjord enveloped us.

Sheer mountains jutted up out of the sea. White-tipped peaks arose skyward, their slopes higher than any I'd seen on the coasts of Norway. Only the Jotunheimens had been taller, but those were inland. The rise from sea level added an extra level of dramatic nature. Nothing could compare to it.

Icy wind blasted past me, threatening to throw me overboard. The boat I was on, an impressive vessel in Bergen harbor, was completely dwarfed and rendered insignificant by this colossal environ.

RAFFAEL CORONELLI

The story of the Sognefjord takes us back to the ice age. In this grim and frostbitten eon, great glaciers wedged into the western side of the Scandinavian peninsula like battle axes with blades kilometers long.

They tore the coastline asunder as they bore inland from the ocean, finding previously-eroded paths in western mountains already raised higher by tectonic shifts. The glaciers gouged further until these inter-mountain ravines became deeper, with sheerer precipices at their sides. When they receded, the glaciers left battle scars in their wake — the fjords. The biggest and deepest remnant of this ravaging geologic onslaught is the mighty Sognefjord, a 205-kilometer gash into western Norway.

I headed back below decks to rest to get out of the wind. The two German women behind me went up to see for themselves. Jagged edges of the fjord flowed by our tiny vessel, out of scale in this majestic realm.

The boat made several stops in the Sognefjord. I'd decided to stay in Balestrand due to its reputation for being a scenic destination with lots of hiking trails, but the other towns wedged into the fjord side seem like idyllic locales.

HOW TO HAVE AN ADVENTURE IN SCANDINAVIA

    The fjord's vastness proved to harbor something big on at least one occasion. In November of 1972, a mysterious submarine was confirmed to have entered the Sognefjord. The Norwegian navy engaged in a heated pursuit. The chase lasted two weeks, winding through the vast crevices in the mountains, the submarine able to dive deep into the fjord's abyssal depths. The chase ended with the submarine escaping into the sea. The Norwegian Navy presumed it to be a Soviet sub, but this was never confirmed. The episode ended without incident.
    Nearing 8pm, the view up from the waters of the Sognefjord was still dramatic. The next stop was mine, so I headed up to the deck for a final look.
    Out on the deck, I ran into the two German women who'd been sitting behind me. I asked what part of Germany they were from. They replied that they were from Hamburg, in northern Germany — just below Scandinavia. The two of them were headed to Sogndal, further down from fjord from where my stop was. We wished each other well on our trips just as the speaker announced that the next stop would be Balestrand.
    This would be our only brief interaction, but it's always nice to meet nice people doing something similar to what you are.

RAFFAEL CORONELLI

From the *Tyrving*'s bow, I saw a miniature side-fjord — Esefjord. On its corner was a town, an old fashioned hotel looking outward to the Sognefjord's rolling waves.

Gathering my bag below decks, I watched us pull in to the dock. The starboard side hatch opened and I exited the ramp onto land.

There was no activity in this small, sleepy town. Above and around me, the mountains of the fjord loomed. I was in the middle of the Norwegian wilds. A sign helpfully pointed the way up from the dock to the town's biggest landmark, the place I'd stay for the next two nights.

The Kviknes Hotel sits at the best spot in town, looking out across the way to the other side of the Sognefjord. An inn existed on the site as far back as the 17th Century. The current main building, finished in 1913, has balconies facing directly onto the fjord. I was lucky enough to have booked a room in this building. The hotel was a destination for everyone from the earliest tourists to the region to visiting foreign royalty.

Kviknes Hotel in Balestrand

HOW TO HAVE AN ADVENTURE IN SCANDINAVIA

Kviknes was my splurge of the trip, the most expensive hotel with the most to offer. Remember what I said about getting what you pay for in a hotel? Kviknes delivered, and it wasn't even absurd in price. It's an excellent hotel in an unbeatable locale — and, as I was about to find out, they treat guests like royalty (and historically, they sometimes were).

Checking in, I was told by the woman at the desk that the kitchens were about to close. I took that as a cue to grab dinner at the lobby bar. A nice, professional bartender took my order of a Hansa and a "Sognefjord Smørbrød".

Called "smorrebrød" in Denmark, where they're essentially the national dish, smørbrød are open-faced sandwiches. Eaten throughout Scandinavia with varying regularity, this one was particularly location-specific. The tiny shrimp topping it were caught locally in the Sognefjord. It was the perfect nighttime welcome meal to my fjordside accommodation.

RAFFAEL CORONELLI

The Sognefjord from a room balcony at the Kviknes Hotel

Finished with dinner, I headed up to my charming room. The old fashioned decor might not be up to everyone's modern standards, but I loved it. Opening the balcony doors, I stepped out to the most unbeatable view — the other side of the Sognefjord.

It was Mother's Day in the US, so I FaceTimed my family and showed them the room, regaling them with highlights of the trip thus far.

I didn't close the shades that night. Nothing could stop me from looking out at that view across the fjord. Mountain peaks beckoned, the low-hanging sun shimmering on the water until it finally descended. Days were longer there than anywhere else thus far. It was the furthest north I'd ever been.

From my bed, I watched the mountains, wondering what secrets they held. The next day, I'd find out.

Balestrand:
The Sognefjord Wilds

Snow-capped mountains above shimmering waters greeted me as I awoke. Normally, I'll reach for my phone upon waking up and check to see if I have any messages or notifications — a dismal habit, but one that I've gotten used to. In Balestrand, the first things I reached for were my glasses. Rather than at a phone screen, the first place I compulsively had to look was out the window.

Being a hotel upwards of a hundred years old, the Kviknes has some archaic elements — notably the design of the bathrooms. A sink stood in the main living area, while the shower/bathtub and toilet were behind a door. Shaving at the mirror over the sink with the spacious room and window to the fjord in the background made me feel like a fancy, old-timey gentleman. The shower and other plumbing still worked perfectly and were outfitted with all the comforts of a modern hotel.

Descending the wooden staircase from the second floor, I traversed the hotel toward the dining hall. Kviknes is decorated in a style that combines high-end Victorian era luxury with muted Nordic aesthetics. Colors are warm and earthy, full of natural wood furnishings. Art inspired by the Viking era adorns the walls alongside landscape paintings that match the sights of the region. A sitting area opens onto a patio overlooking the fjord, the hotel making full use of its unbeatable view.

RAFFAEL CORONELLI

Interior of the Kviknes Hotel

I heeded the sign by the dining hall's entrance and waited to be seated. A man thanked me for waiting before showing me to a table next to a window. I accepted his offer for coffee, and got up to peruse the buffet.

Breakfast at the Kvikness was my first taste of an old-fashioned full Nordic breakfast smorgasbord. At least three different types of pickled herring in various sauces were available, so I naturally had to try them all. They were the perfect way to begin a day in the Norwegian wilderness, as were the smoked locks (salmon). Other pickled things included mushrooms and cucumbers. Like Japan, Scandinavia has fishy traditional breakfasts, which may be atypical for some. I certainly didn't mind, but there were plenty of other things to choose from.

While refilling my coffee, the breakfast waiter asked where I was from. I replied Chicago, and he remarked that I must've traveled a long way. I told him where I'd been up to that point, to which he listened with interest. I get the impression that most guests at Kviknes are from Norway, and others from other parts of Europe.

HOW TO HAVE AN ADVENTURE IN SCANDINAVIA

Oslo and Bergen have tourists from everywhere, but I'd reached a more remote part of the country.

The breakfast waiter asked what I was doing that day, to which I said hiking, prompting a reply.

"Don't do Raudmelen this time of year unless you have snow shoes. You'll be in snow up to your waist."

I thanked him for the advice, since I certainly didn't want to be in snow up to my waist. I asked if the other trails were alright, to which he assured me that they were.

Service at Kviknes really does make you feel fancy. I'm not putting down service elsewhere in Norway, but the people at that hotel make your experience special.

Bidding farewell to the breakfast waiter, he wished me well on my day's adventure. At that, I stopped by the room to grab my backpack (including the absolutely needed huge water bottle I'd bought) and then the front desk to gather one last piece of information.

The front desk at the Kviknes has maps to and around the local hiking trails. You can find this information online, but I wasn't sure where to begin looking for it and my phone reception was not reliable enough to trust that I wouldn't have gotten lost. The person at the desk was happy to point me through town to the trailhead.

Sunlight shining, it was a beautiful day in the Sognefjord. Thus, I slathered myself in sunscreen. The poncho was in my backpack in case it rained, but I wouldn't end up needing it. It's still a good idea to bring things like that in case of emergency.

The route I'd have to take along winding neighborhood streets alerted me to something I hadn't realized. For a place with such a prominent hotel as a major historic landmark, Balestrand is not made for tourists. This is not a downside, but in fact makes it interesting — it's a residential town that you have to walk through to get to the mountain trails.

RAFFAEL CORONELLI

Balestrand

Setting off through the town, I passed a modern reconstruction of a stave church. This was built fairly recently and was not a historic piece. I continued up the hillside into a residential neighborhood. Houses overlooked the fjord from the hillside at the mountain's foot. There were no other people on the roads on this bright, sunny day. This was the vibe of Balestrand — sleepy, quietly laying in the shadow of nature that dwarfs it from all around.

Rounding the final corner up a hill to which signs marking the nature trails pointed, I came across the ultimate indication that these facilities were not made with tourists in mind. A building that I at first thought was some type of visitor center lay next to the trailhead's entrance. It's a good thing I didn't try to go inside before I realized its true purpose. It was a primary school. For some reason, the entrance to the trails is from the school's parking lot.

Stepping up to the trailhead, I read the sign and compared its options to the trail map I'd received from the hotel desk. It listed trails by length and elevation change.

HOW TO HAVE AN ADVENTURE IN SCANDINAVIA

Raudmelen was the one I'd been warned was still covered in snow, as it goes up to the mountaintop. Buråsi is the next highest, going up 575 meters in elevation. I chose to do the third highest, Balabu, ascending 400 meters in elevation to the Balabu way station.

For comparison, Fløyen's peak in Bergen was 400 meters above sea level, and I took a funicular most of the way up the mountain. To reach Balabu, I'd be doing a rugged hike the equivalent to walking from the base of Fløyen all the way to its summit, sans any kind of vehicular assistance. This was the type of thing for which I'd come to Balestrand.

Winding up the main trail for a little while, I began the hike. The trail branched off, pointing upwards. A gate marked the entrance to the higher, more challenging route, marked with an inscription to keep it closed so as to not allow mountain wildlife to wander into the town. A sign pointed the way past the gate to Raudmelen, and to my destination, Balabu.

The gate creaked as I opened it and stepped through, venturing upward along the steep route. Around rocky crags it wound, past alternating vistas onto the Esefjord to the northwest and the Sognefjord to the south.

RAFFAEL CORONELLI

Balestrand and the Sognefjord

I stopped and stood for a minute in the middle of the trail overlooking the Sognefjord through the trees. Birds chirped over faint sounds of the town far below. I took a breath of crisp mountain air, the only smells those of the forest. The sun filtered through the branches. I made a note to remember the feeling of this place.

A little further up, I found a bench on an overlook, dangerously close to a precarious drop-off. If one were to slip off the bench, they'd fall off the cliff — maybe not optimal placement for safety, but great for thrill-seekers.

Continuing upwards, I followed the signs to Balabu. A stream crossed the trail, dropping off into a waterfall below. I stopped for another brief respite, watching its endless flow from the mountaintop above to the fjord beneath. I was much higher now.

The path twisted over and around rocks and roots. The forest gradually thinned the higher on the mountain I got. My water bottle saw heavy use, and soon I'd drank most of it. Luckily, I'd have a refill coming sooner than I'd have expected.

HOW TO HAVE AN ADVENTURE IN SCANDINAVIA

Balabu way station

My boots crunched against a new kind of terrain — snow. The trees had fallen away, and I was at the point on the mountain where the snow-capped peak was about to start. This was as far as I'd been advised to ascend. Just as I was prepared to turn back, I noticed something over the next pile of snow — a small house in the last patch of grass this high on the mountain, at the edge of a steep cliff.

Climbing up, I found myself at the Balabu way station — the point to which the trail had been taking me.

Bada bing, Balabu! I thought to myself.

(I don't know why, that's just what was in my head at the time.)

A tiny house on the vast mountain, the way station at Balabu is a free-to-use hut owned and maintained by the Norwegian park service.

RAFFAEL CORONELLI

Balabu way station interior

I was shocked at how well furnished it was for something in such a remote and inaccessible place. Outside on the appealingly designed entry porch was a large jug of mountain water for water bottles, which I promptly used to refill mine. There was also an axe, presumably to chop wood to build a fire at the nearby fire pit — or whatever purpose for which visitors to a secluded hut on a mountain in the Norwegian wilderness should want to use an axe.

The inside was even more shockingly inviting. A sign on the door instructs visitors to remove hiking boots when stepping inside. Wooden benches and a loft-like bunk were situated around the rim. Shelves with books lined the wall.

I'd imagine the use for a place like this would be if the weather were to become inhospitable, and hiking down from the mountain became dangerous.

HOW TO HAVE AN ADVENTURE IN SCANDINAVIA

Staying in this cozy hut might not be the Kviknes, but it seems more than accommodating. The axe, the cliff, and the inaccessible locale would also make it a great murder setting, but please behave yourselves and refrain from bringing enemies there.

For my purposes, the Balabu way station was the perfect place to sit and rest after the long walk up. Gulping down cool mountain water from my refilled bottle, I gazed down from the wooden bench built into the outside of the hut onto Balestrand and the Sognefjord far below. Wind blew across the mountaintop. Snow and ice lay just beside where the hut resided.

I'd climbed 400 meters up the mountain. Only the inaccessible peak of Raudmelen was above me. The human realm was below, crisp high-altitude air filling my lungs. In this remote place, I'd once again found the sublime.

Balabu was the type of place I imagined when I decided I wanted to go into the Norwegian wilderness on this wing of the trip. It was a reward for the arduous climb, an idyllic place that one must ascend the mountain to reach.

I wanted to stay, but I still had the climb down ahead. Water bottle refilled, I crossed the patch of snow and left Balabu way station behind. The rustic hut grew smaller behind me until it was obscured by the mountainside.

For someone who was still dealing with a pulled ligament in my knee, the climb up had been no problem at all. The climb down was a bit more difficult in terms of having to move my leg certain ways, but I was always careful to keep my balance. A fall to my death would certainly be an unpleasant addition to such a nice day.

Around and down the mountain the trail wound until I was back at the gate. Closing it behind me, I moved on to the next part of my day on the mountainside.

RAFFAEL CORONELLI

It still wasn't noon yet — maybe I could've stayed at Balabu way station for a bit longer — but I figured I could go on another, less strenuous hike.

Following the sign to the "Naturstien" trail, I went on a pleasant, relatively level walk along the lower part of the mountain that took up the remainder of the morning. Sign posts along the way talked about local flora and fauna. Through the trees, Balestrand was just below.

Emerging from the forest, I returned to the town proper to see if there was anything to do in the afternoon, like shops or some other attraction.

I soon found confirmation of what I'd thought that morning. Balestrand is not made for tourists.

Furthermore, it was a Tuesday and for whatever reason, even things like cafes were closed. I wasn't hungry, as the luxurious breakfast had been enough to get me through to dinner, but it was still strange to stroll through a town at noon and find absolutely nothing open.

I decided to walk up the street on the Esefjord side of town to see if I ran into anything interesting. After walking a bit and admiring the towering peaks at the end of Esefjord from the shore beneath them, I turned around and headed back to the area of Balestrand near the hotel.

A harbor where private boats could dock was near a small park with benches. Nearby was a sign for the small Sognefjord Aquarium, which sounds like it might be a nice attraction when it's open. It wasn't. Otherwise, the sleepy town of Balestrand was in a deep midday slumber.

Then a thought occurred to me — where were all the older people staying at the hotel? The Kviknes seemed to be a hit with elderly Norwegians when I was at breakfast, but they were nowhere to be found during the day. Where had they disappeared to? I wasn't about to go looking for them, but I found it strange that a whole population of visitors were in the immediate vicinity and yet the town was devoid of them — or anyone else, for that matter.

HOW TO HAVE AN ADVENTURE IN SCANDINAVIA

Esefjord

Having wandered around a shuttered Balestrand for an hour or so, I decided there was only one thing left to do — go back to the trailhead and go for another hike. I'd opt for another easier trail as my knee was still slightly bothering me and I'd already made my day while doing a harder one in the morning. It was, after all, my reason for going there.

Climbing back up the road to the trailhead, a swarm of children advanced toward me. The school by the trails had let out just in time for me to return to that spot. Not wanting to seem like a menace, I minded my own business and moved through the crowd to the trailhead. The sign once again pointed toward the trails while I consulted the map I'd gotten to decide which one to take.

I'd already done the nature trail, so I chose Skåsheim, another low-lying trail around the mountainside with little change in elevation. I wouldn't go the full five kilometers of the loop, but it was doable for the afternoon and would allow me to go as far as I liked before turning back.

Once I was out on the trail, any frustration left me. The mountainside was peaceful. Views of the Sognefjord peeked through the trees at various intervals.

There was one main difference in this low-level hike — bugs. Insects were scarce further up the mountain, but in the more densely forested areas further down, I encountered exponentially more flying insects. I'd brought insect repellent for this purpose and quickly applied it.

By the time I'd finished the hike, it was late afternoon and time to return to the hotel. As I walked through the sleepy town, I saw my first signs of life — people returning home, walking along the streets, saying hello to each other. It wasn't bustling by any stretch of the imagination, but it had life in it. Balestrand was a place where people lived in the shadow on the Sognefjord's majesty. They were quiet, perhaps by the nature of the place in which they lived.

Back at the hotel at 5:00PM, I headed for the bar. It'd been a hefty day of three mountain hikes and four crosstown treks. I deserved a smooth glass of Norwegian akvavit.

I asked the bartender what the aquavit selection was. She rolled out the bottles, both major labels and smaller local varieties. I chose one of the big names I hadn't yet tried — Linie.

Sitting down with my glass, I took a sip and felt the waters of the Sognefjord splash against my tastebuds. Linie is a traditional Norwegian style aquavit. I'd compare it to the Gammel I had, with light caraway and star anise flavors and a touch of sweetness. It was a lovely, refreshing treat after the day's strenuous exploits. Aquavit's name comes from "aqua vitae," which means "water of life" in Latin. This glass certainly had that feeling.

HOW TO HAVE AN ADVENTURE IN SCANDINAVIA

Linie proclaims on its bottle that it's "matured at sea", like the original Norwegian style akvavit that aged longer than intended due to the length of the voyage it was on. It was also the brand brought on the Fram when it sailed into the Arctic and Antarctic, the drink of choice of Roald Amundsen and his Norwegian explorers. Something about that prestige adds to the experience of drinking it, especially after my own activities that day.

The hotel restaurant was the only open restaurant in town to which I wanted to go. I'm now glad I was forced in my choice, as I cannot possibly imagine another option having been as good. Dinner began at 7:00PM, so I had about an hour and a half to kill after my pre-dinner drink. To kill time, I decided to make use of part of my room that I hadn't gotten a chance to utilize — the private balcony.

The front of the Kviknes' historic main building really does have the best possible view in Balestrand. Exhausted, I had a comfortable chair on which to sit and enjoy it.

I could've complained more about the lack of things to do in Balestrand, but that would be missing the point. This was a place to go to get away from having to do any of that. The itinerary had been the hiking trails, and my reaching the Balabu way station had been the day's grand accomplishment — a 400-meter ascent that outdid any other physical activity on the trip by length and effort. Sitting and watching the waves roll in off the Sognefjord was the opposite, but had a similar reward. It was an escape from the world, and I could do it from the comfort of my hotel room balcony. Maybe that's why the Kviknes is such a hit with older people.

7:00 arrived before I knew it, and I descended to the dining hall. I was one of the first to enter, seated by the maitre d' next to the window with another glorious view of the fjord. My waiter was the same one from breakfast.

RAFFAEL CORONELLI

"Good evening, sir! How were your hikes today?" he asked, still friendly and with genuine interest.

"Great!" I replied. "I went up to Balabu. It's incredible up there."

He handed me a menu that was really more of a guide to the set menu for the evening after confirming my lack of dietary restrictions. I'd be having fjord trout, caught right out in the Sognefjord on which my table overlooked.

The drink to accompany it would be my choice. I went with a Løiten, another major Norwegian akvavit to cross off the list. Aged in sherry barrels on cargo ships, Løiten is one of the oldest types of Norwegian aquavit and provides a bit of a stronger taste than the standard Linie I'd had thanks to the choice of barrel in which it's matured.

It wasn't long before my fjord trout arrived. The presentation was exquisite, a fish steak done to perfection, topped with a light cream sauce and an assortment of neatly arranged greens. The fish itself was a bright orange, looking more like salmon than trout. I have to wonder if this was because of the trout's diet out in the fjord, remembering the tiny shrimp I'd had the last night.

Right:
Fjord Trout
at the Kviknes Hotel

HOW TO HAVE AN ADVENTURE IN SCANDINAVIA

Taking my first bite, the spoils of the Sognefjord ignited my tastebuds. Tastefully rich, but not overly, the fjord trout transported me to the deck of a ship like the *Hordagut*, the fishing trawler I'd seen docked in Bergen. It took me back further to the northern fishermen of the 19th and early 20th Centuries, the time in which the Kviknes hotel was built, whose boats still bore the construction style of Viking longships. I watched the waves between the mountains out the window, savoring what they'd brought.

The Løiten complemented the meal perfectly. Its own oceanic developmental process gave a seafaring theme to the combination of tastes.

Dessert consisted of a small pastry. A creation of the chef, it was a delicate confection and a nice way to end the evening.

The Kviknes restaurant was one of the best I went to in Norway. If you're staying in the hotel, or even nearby, it's more than worth seeking out a meal there. The food, service, and view from the table made me feel like royalty. I can't imagine there being a better restaurant on the Sognefjord.

The waiter asked if I'd like to add the restaurant tab to my hotel room bill, to which I agreed — a certain perk of staying in the hotel. I thanked him profusely for such good service at both breakfast and dinner.

Heading back up through the exquisitely decorated hotel to my room, I thought back on what a good day it had been. It was a different pace than the others, but in its own way, it was exactly what I wanted from Balestrand.

If you don't mind doing nothing between extensive hiking and staying in your luxurious hotel, Balestrand is a fine spot to stay in one of the most picturesque locales in the world. Maybe there's more to do when you're not there on a Tuesday when everything is shuttered, or at least the Sognefjord Aquarium isn't being renovated.

Otherwise, it's a sleepy residential town in rural Norway with the staggering vista of the Sognefjord looming perennially in its background like the pantheon of the Norse gods watching over the mundanity of the world below. That has its own appeal — and the hotel and restaurant were experiences in themselves.

I once again fell asleep with the shades open. The Sognefjord was out there, and I wasn't going to miss a single second of looking at it.

Suburban Bergen:
Tales of Ashes and Trolls

Just before heading up to bed the previous night, I mentioned to the front desk that my boat back to Bergen was leaving the dock at 7:50 AM. Breakfast is normally served at either 7:00 or 7:30, so I inquired if I'd be able to have it before leaving to make the boat. The receptionist replied that a full breakfast plate would be waiting for me in the bar at 7:00, conveniently ready to go so that I could eat it and then dash out. Kviknes treated me like a king.

I took one last look out the window of my room before I headed down. Nothing would beat this view.

Sure enough, a breakfast plate was waiting for me in the bar. It had all the staples — locks, pickled herring, eggs, fruits, etc.

Outside, a grey-blue sky and rain announced the type of day it would be. The previous day's hikes had lucked out.

This had been the nicest hotel at which I'd stayed on the trip, and would comfortably retain that designation. It was a short walk from the Kviknes down to the dock where I'd catch the express boat back to Bergen.

Balestrand harbor in rain

RAFFAEL CORONELLI

The Tyrving approaches the Balestrand dock

Before long, an aerodynamic shape approached on the dark water. Its side read *Tyrving*, the same boat that had brought me to Balestrand the day before last.

I boarded and grabbed a seat in the same area I'd sat on the way there. This time, I had a view of the south side of the Sognefjord, submerged in far spookier weather. Something about the elements crashing around the boat in this vast place made sitting in its spacious cabin feel warmer. Rain pelted the window and the choppy water beyond, storm clouds hanging low over the mountain peaks on either side of the *Tyrving* as it pulled away from Balestrand and into the storm on the fjord.

I decided I could use another coffee, so I got up to see if the machine was still out of order. To my pleasant surprise, it was in working order. This is when I made my oblivious and rather embarrassing mistake.

This was indeed the same coffee machine that had been free to use in the Bergensbanen's first class. By that estimation, I thought, this one must be as well. As I began returning to my seat with my coffee, an older woman behind the concessions counter next to the coffee machine called after me in Norwegian.

"Unnskylde," I said. "Snakker du engelsk?"
"Are you going to pay for that?" she prodded.
"Oh!" I said in surprise. "How much is it?"

HOW TO HAVE AN ADVENTURE IN SCANDINAVIA

Inside the Tyrving on the rainy Sognefjord

I went up to the counter and paid the roughly four dollar charge for the coffee.

NORLED, I learned, is not like first class on the Bergensbanen despite having identical coffee machines.

"Did you think it was for free?!" she said in disbelief as if I'd tried to shoplift an Armani suit.

"Well, it's just there..." I trailed off, realizing my explanation wasn't going to cut it.

The woman smiled a tense, passive-aggressive grin through gritted teeth. I'd know from then on not to take the coffee. Hopefully you can learn from my mistake.

Settled into my seat with a coffee that cost more than I'd expected, I gazed out the window at the stormblåst (storm cloud) over the Sognefjord in all its dark majesty. It'd looked amazing in broad daylight, but seeing it in starkly different weather made for a novel journey.

A few hours more of barreling through the storm and the *Tyrving* had left the Sognefjord behind. Byfjorden waited for its arrival, and at its back, shrouded in the gloom through which I'd first laid eyes on it, was Bergen.

Out my port side window, Bryggen lined up to welcome the ship's arrival. Shrouded in rain and darkness, the colorful wooden buildings were far eerier than they'd been on the sunny days on which I'd visited them.

My umbrella went up again as I disembarked. Through splashing puddles on the sidewalks, I made a B-line for the tram station at the Byparken stop.

Byparken is the end of the #1 tram line, or the beginning, depending on your direction. This line goes between central Bergen and the airport. I was headed out to the west suburbs for the day and staying near the airport, so I bought a 24-hour pass on the Bergen Skyss ticket app.

The tram set off through Bergen's neighborhoods to the southwest. This was my first taste of the city outside of the compact center.

One of the tram stops bore an amusing name — "Florida". This is not a Norwegian word, and does come from the US state. From what I can gather, the "Florida" area in Bergen may have been named for a 19th Century restauranteur in the area.

"This isn't the Florida I know," a Norwegian man joked to his friend in English as we passed the stop.

Indeed, sunny Florida this was not. Overhead gloom dominated the skies and a steady drizzle hit the windows. At least it wasn't quite a Florida hurricane. Ironic, somewhat, that Bergen's weather is brought up by the Gulf Stream, which originates near Florida.

The #1 tram line will take you (more or less) to both of the attractions I'll talk about in this chapter. I went back to see them, because lugging my bag around with me was not something I wanted to do all day. I rode the tram all the way to the end of the line and got off at the airport station.

Once topside, I followed the signs by the airport directing me to my hotel — the Scandic Flesland.

HOW TO HAVE AN ADVENTURE IN SCANDINAVIA

Scandic are in pretty much every Scandinavian city, so if you want a reliable alternative to some of the less luxurious hotels I stayed in, you can't go wrong with these. Think of something on the level of a Marriott — nice enough, standardized, and giving you what you pay for. They also stand apart from other western hotel chains by incorporating elements of modern Scandinavian design into every part of them.

Closing my umbrella and stepping into the circular lobby, I asked the front desk if I could check in yet despite being several hours early. To my surprise, the woman at the desk said that my room was ready, and directed me toward it. Ascending in a glass elevator that spoke to me in Norwegian with a pre-recorded woman's voice, I knew I'd chosen a good hotel and wasn't in store for a cost-cutting budget affair like the ones in Oslo and Bergen's center.

The view out the window of my room was the polar opposite of the one I'd had at the Kviknes, a long-distance view of the airport runway. That didn't matter. What I needed from this hotel was a comfortable base of operations for my last day of sightseeing in the Bergen area, and a place from which to leave in the morning for my flight north.

Leaving my larger bag in the room, I headed back out to the airport tram station. I was on my way to two distinct sights of historic cultural importance in Bergen's southwest suburbia.

The rain did not let up as the tram took me back northeast. My first destination was in a park at the southwest edge of Bergen proper, a sight of architectural interest and a tumultuous story that serves as a sort of coda to my visit to Neseblod Records in Oslo.

Arriving at Fantoft station, I opened my umbrella and stepped out onto the wet platform. A foreboding atmosphere that might not have been there on a sunny day set the tone for where I was about to go.

RAFFAEL CORONELLI

Taking a series of left turns on the winding Fantoftvegen, I followed the left hand path through an unassuming suburban district.

A funereal vibe permeated the dark atmosphere as rain fell against my black umbrella. Dread hung in the air. I'd picked the perfect day to visit Fantoft.

A sign reading "Fantoft Stavkirke" pointed off the main road and into a path through a forest park. I followed it, and soon the woods surrounded me. The path wound down a hill, the trees obscuring something — a black, jagged shape watching from the forest.

The trees cleared, revealing the sepulchral figure.

Standing at the center of the clearing was an obsidian black wooden building in the shape of a serrated shroud. Points like blades reached up toward the storm cloud, each depicting a black dragon.

Fantoft Stave Church

HOW TO HAVE AN ADVENTURE IN SCANDINAVIA

In that weather, through a grim filter and a low light level that darkened its surface from brighter pictures I'd seen, Fantoft Stave Church was one of the most sinister looking buildings I'd ever seen. Contributing to that, of course, was my knowledge of it.

The initial iteration of the stavkirke was built in the Viking age. Over the centuries, it was moved and restored a number of times, even leaving its original foundation in Sogn to a new one in Bergen in the 19th Century where it was rebuilt to the specifications of 11th Century architecture. The most recent reconstruction was completed in 1997.

This would all be normal for a Norwegian stave church. What set this one apart visually, other than the darkness in which I viewed it, was the fence surrounding its perimeter.

I peered through the chain links. A sign hung at eye level indicating that a security camera was filming.

RAFFAEL CORONELLI

Fantoft Stave Church and grounds

A stone cross protruded from a mound of earth in front of the church at an off-kilter angle. Moved to the church yard from the town of Tjora upon the building's relocation to Bergen in the 1880s, its haphazard positioning made it appear as if someone stuck it into the ground at that spot in a panic.

The fence gave off the vibe of either a prison or a closed carnival ride. In summer months (after late May), you can pay an admission fee to see the inside of it.

HOW TO HAVE AN ADVENTURE IN SCANDINAVIA

When closed, as it was on the day of my visit, the heavily secured barrier felt as much like it was keeping something in as keeping people out. It was as if some specter resided in its volcanic-rock-colored timbers. Behind that containment fence raged a silent battle.

Fantoft Stave Church's previous iteration burned down in 1992. The arsonist responsible, known by a variety of names including Count Grishnackh, was later sent to prison for another act — the brutal murder of Euronymous, former owner of the record store I visited in Oslo and lead guitarist of the band with whom the murderer had a brief stint as a replacement bass player.

I circled the outside, taking in the jagged form from all angles. The burning, the stabbing of Mayhem's guitarist — it all hung in the air around this place, even though the latter event happened elsewhere. Maybe it would've felt different in sunnier weather. Maybe it was fortuitous that it didn't.

RAFFAEL CORONELLI

Fantoft Stavkirke

HOW TO HAVE AN ADVENTURE IN SCANDINAVIA

An Italian family walked up to the fence and took photos. Did they know the place's story? Would it even matter to them?

In a less esoteric light, it's just an interesting building with ties to a strange incident. The fact that it's rebuilt isn't anything abnormal. The golden pagoda Kinkaku-ji in Kyoto famously burned down by arson and was rebuilt in the mid-20th Century, and no one will say it's worse off.

The one currently moved to the Cultural History Museum in Oslo is itself mostly a new construction despite its status of being "original". Images of what the Fantoft church looked like in the 19th Century already suggest drastic prior changes. As I stated in the section on the Norsk Folkemuseum, thousand-year-old wooden buildings must have their materials replaced as they deteriorate.

Of course, doing it all at once isn't usually the preferred method. Bergen's own Abbath, who was uninvolved in these incidents despite the subsequent hysteria surrounding Norway's Black Metal scene, pointed out in a hilarious televised interview he conducted in full stage getup that the Norwegian government uses taxpayers' money to restore damaged historic sites.

Fantoft Stavkirke is still an imposing example of 11th Century architecture possibly based on older Norse Godhouses, a notion bolstered by evidence like the University of Bergen's find in the Sunnmøre region. Established amidst historic tumult, it perhaps fits that its modern legacy includes some as well.

Fantoft is worth a look if you're in the area and harbor any (possibly morbid) curiosity. It was something I had to check out, a pitch black specter onto which I'm glad to have gazed in person.

Back at the tram station, the rain let up and the sun emerged. It set a different and just as appropriate tone for the afternoon's second destination to the southwest — a place that belonged to one of Norway's most revered sons.

RAFFAEL CORONELLI

Left:
Tram Line 1 approaches Hop station

Hopping off the tram at Hop station (sorry), I started my walk west through the residential neighborhood where resides the former residence turned museum of Norway's most famous classical composer, Edvard Grieg. His home, in a name that reminds one of his association with a certain mythological creature, was Troldhaugen.

I operate these books under the inference that people can follow in my footsteps to have as good a trip as I did, or learn from my mistakes and do the opposite. The following statement falls into the latter category. If you don't want to embark on a complex walking route that will take near a half hour if you don't get lost, consider taking a cab to Troldhaugen.

The tram simply does not drop you off close to Grieg's estate, with near two kilometers of winding residential streets in between. Looking back, of course, that was all part of the adventure.

The sun was now fully out in Bergen's suburb Paradis. The darkness of my visit to Fantoft had passed, and Paradis emerged bright and welcoming, though also very confusing.

Following the map on my phone without GPS due to lack of signal, I wound up and around twisting roads and through roundabouts, trying to stay on Troldhaugvegen.

HOW TO HAVE AN ADVENTURE IN SCANDINAVIA

At last, signs marked "Troldhaugen" began to appear at the roadside, instilling confidence that I was indeed going the right way. The hill of the trolls was near.

Troldhaugen does indeed mean "troll hill" in Old Norse. This is very much thematically in line with Grieg's interest in Nordic folklore, trolls, and folk music.

His most famous work, the orchestral soundtrack to the fairy tale-based play *Peer Gynt,* brought creatures and landscapes of Norwegian folklore to the world's attention at the end of the 19th century and influenced the global perception of Nordic traditions; it's no exaggeration to say that Grieg's popularizing of these elements shaped modern notions of Northern European folklore and lay the foundations for the Fantasy genre as we know it.

A bushy black and white cat walked across the street and stopped at the roadside. A cat! I'll always stop what I'm doing to say hello to a cat. Did it understand English, or only Norwegian? Such questions always come to mind. It looked at me with some interest before dashing off into the yard of a nearby house, perhaps where it lived.

173

Past the cat and a few more houses was the entrance to Troldhaugen.

The grounds included a museum on Grieg's life, where one pays admission to the estate. Beyond it were the concert hall, and Grieg's house and garden.

The first stop, by necessity of containing the admissions office, was the modern museum building. Admission came with an audio guide for the house and grounds. The museum exhibit was a general history of Grieg's life, containing personal artifacts and ones related to his compositions.

Grieg's Hardanger fiddle was on display in a case. This Norwegian folk instrument saw use as part of his desire to reconnect with and amplify Norway's history of folk music. Grieg studied and collected Norwegian folk songs, transcribing and arranging them for performance. This legacy allowed obscure folk music of the region to see wide enjoyment, helping to popularize Norway's traditional culture around the world. His *Norwegian Dances* suites contain a number of these uncovered gems.

Folk music wasn't the only extent of Grieg's fascination with uncovering the folk culture of the country in which he lived. He also held a fascination with folktales, especially those of mythical creatures like trolls.

His friend Henrik Ibsen played into this interest when he tapped Grieg to compose the musical score for his play, *Peer Gynt*. In the play, the title character descends into a mountain cave that turns out to be ruled by trolls.

This section of the play features what is ultimately Grieg's single most enduring composition — "In the Hall of the Mountain King." The jumpy, vaguely sinister melody that starts small and gradually builds into a majestic choral piece left an indelible mark on music we now associate with creatures of the dark. Danny Elfman noticeably got most of his signature musical style from this composition.

HOW TO HAVE AN ADVENTURE IN SCANDINAVIA

Edvard Grieg's house at Troldhaugen

RAFFAEL CORONELLI

Incidentally, I'd seen a live performance of *Peer Gynt* with an orchestra about a month and a half before the trip, with my sister playing principal harp in the Milwaukee Symphony. This was a great primer for going to Grieg's estate, as well as the various troll-related places I'd visit in Norway.

Grieg kept a small doll of a troll to which, according to his wife, he would say "goodnight" each night before going to sleep. This eccentric personal item was on display in the museum, and gave a window of intimacy to Grieg's composition. He wasn't just making music about monsters — he empathized with and loved the trolls.

Right: Grieg's troll doll

HOW TO HAVE AN ADVENTURE IN SCANDINAVIA

Between the museum and Grieg's house lies a bridge. This might seem normal, but given his appreciation for Norwegian trolls, it's worth mentioning their connection with bridges.

Trolls residing under bridges is a theme that emerged with a 19th Century translation of a Norwegian folktale — "Three Billy Goats Gruff." In this story, which you've likely heard in some version, three goats have to cross a bridge under which lives a carnivorous troll who wants to eat them. This story, via its English translation, became popular around the same time Grieg was writing his music based on Norwegian folk songs, tales, and trolls. It has absolutely nothing to do with the bridge by Grieg's house, but it's fun to imagine that a troll might live in such a place due to its former owner's affinity for them.

I crossed the bridge without being eaten by a troll. On the other side was a two-story house built in a typical 19th Century style, with light cream colored walls and a veranda overlooking the garden. The view from the garden looks out onto Byfjorden, a visual that inspired Grieg while writing.

A drawing of a troll in Grieg's house

RAFFAEL CORONELLI

Left:
Interior of Grieg's house at Troldhaugen

Inside the house were a trove of artifacts and furnishings. Most of the open rooms were decorated as they were when Grieg had lived there, with the front room housing some pictures of his own personage. Books of sheet music he'd written lay next to one of his pianos, thick volumes in which he'd painstakingly scrawled compositions by hand. Over a doorway hung a drawing of a giant troll standing in the middle of a town — a fine art piece emblematic of his fixation on the creatures.

Just a few meters from the house, overlooking the fjord, was a small cabin. In it was a grand piano and stacks of written compositions. This was Grieg's composition hut, where he'd go to experience utter seclusion and write music on his piano while looking out at Byfjorden.

It must've worked, because he apparently spent copious amounts of time there, undisturbed. This private office reminded me a bit of Balabu way station, but not as high up and closer to its user's home.

The other main building on the premises was a concert hall. There was no concert that afternoon, but when there is, it overlooks the same view Grieg would've seen from his composer's hut. Chamber music and piano concerts playing Grieg's music and the older Norwegian folk music he transcribed are held regularly.

HOW TO HAVE AN ADVENTURE IN SCANDINAVIA

A walk down a steep flight of stairs took me to the last place on Troldhaugen's map. On a sheer cliff face, seen from a rocky ledge at the edge of the ocean, is embedded a stone tomb. On it is inscribed letters resembling Norse runes. They read, "Edvard and Nina Grieg."

This is Grieg's tomb, where his ashes rest along with his wife's. It feels suitably like something from a legend, a tomb in a cliffside overlooking Byfjorden. There the "Mountain King" composer rests, inside the hill of the trolls — his eternal friends, whose wonders he showed the world.

Edvard and Nina Grieg's tomb at Troldhaugen

Returning my audio guide at the front desk, I said goodbye to Troldhaugen and left this idyllic estate behind. I'd felt the magic of that place where folklore was captured and put to music. It would not be my last troll-related encounter in Norway.

Getting back to Hop station took just as long as getting there from it, but I managed to find my way. Soon I was seated on the southwest-bound tram to the airport in Flesland.

Back at the Scandic, I took a quick shower before dinner. I'd imagine all Scandic bathrooms are similar, as it seems to be that type of hotel chain. I greatly enjoyed the ultramodern shower design and found it spacious and comfortable. I freshened up and headed down to the hotel restaurant for dinner. The area in which I was staying wasn't exactly restaurant central, and I'd had a tiring day.

The Scandic Flesland's restaurant was Italian. I tend to enjoy sampling what different countries make of another's cuisine. For example, Italian-American food is its own entire universe compared to Italian food from Italy, which is totally different from Japanese-Italian restaurants. In Norway, I found that Italian restaurants are most similar to the ones in Italy, likely because native Italians are fairly easy to get ahold of in Western Europe.

Since a Neapolitan style pizza oven was advertised on the menu, I ordered a pizza capricciosa. I like a good pizza, as I should — I'm from Chicago, home of the deep dish and tavern style pizzas, and have family ties to southern Italy where the first pizzas were forged in the fires of Mt. Vesuvius; so one might say I have pizza sauce in my blood. What would Neapolitan style pizza made in Norway be like? I was eager to taste it and see.

HOW TO HAVE AN ADVENTURE IN SCANDINAVIA

As it turned out, it was a lot like Neapolitan style pizza that's properly made anywhere the chef knows what they're doing. In other words, it was excellent. It wasn't Norwegian food, but it definitely hit the spot and was a good option for an evening after a day full of so much traveling.

It had been one of my fullest days of the trip. I'd sailed from the height of the Sognefjord to Bergen, then gone to Fantoft, to Troldhaugen, and to this hotel by the Bergen airport in Flesland. This day was my coda for the time I'd spent in this part of Norway.

I had an early start the next morning, so I retired to my room and closed the blackout curtains. I wouldn't be staying up to see a sunset.

Where I was going the next day, there would be no sunset to see.

Arctic landscape over Vikran
in the Troms region of Norway

Tromsø:
The Arctic

Due to its proximity to the airport, the hotel opened breakfast at 4:00AM. This was great news for me, as Flesland was indeed my launch point from which I had to make an early flight north.

Scandic's breakfast is described by their own website as "award-winning." I must say, it's excellent. Tons of Scandinavian options lay out from cured meats to pickled herrings and of course locks. I was able to enjoy it in plenty of time. Immediately after, I checked out and headed down the road in the rising sun to the Bergen Flesland Airport.

Flying was necessary for this wing of the trip, as Norway's north-south length is immense. The Arctic coast is as far from Oslo as Oslo is from Italy, if you can believe it. As discussed earlier, a high speed train is impossible due to the fjords blocking a northward land passage. Thus, the only way to pass the Nordland region and into the Troms og Finnmark region is either to take a long sea voyage, or to fly. I chose flying, out of cost and time considerations.

For the sake of convenience, I checked my bag. Checking a bag on a flight with connections can have unfortunate consequences, as I'd discover on the way home, but this was domestic and operated all by the same airline.

RAFFAEL CORONELLI

SAS is a Swedish airline, but operates out of both Norway and Denmark as well. It's part of the Star Alliance, which allowed me to get miles on my ANA mileage account. I had nothing but good experiences on SAS, and would book with them again whenever I return to Scandinavia.

Check in and security were a breeze compared to American airports, as to be expected. Before long, I was by the gate waiting to board the flight north to Trondheim, where I'd make my connection to the extreme north.

While waiting, I plugged in my headphones and listened to the entirety of Immortal's *Battles in the North* album, recorded at Bergen's Grieghallen. The exhilarating riffing psyched me up for the journey as I sat by the gate and watched the runway. Bergen and the Vestland region had been unforgettable. Now, "Grim and Frostbitten Kingdoms" were indeed on the agenda.

The first flight of the day was negligible. Before I knew it, the plane had passed over the Sognefjord and landed at Trondheim. Snowy mountains formed a ring around the city at the top of the Jotunheimen mountain range. I had an hour to kill at Trondheim airport before the second flight.

Though I didn't make a stop there, Trondheim may well be a good destination for a trip to Norway. On an infinite budget and an infinite amount of time, I would've loved to have seen it, and I may still someday.

Trondheim is the last, northernmost vestige of what would constitute "central Norway." It's the last major city you can reasonably get to on a train from Oslo. If you're in Trondheim, you're as far as you can get while still being relatively connected. Further north lies Nordland, a scenic region that straddles the arctic circle. Even beyond that was my destination in the Troms og Finnmark region.

HOW TO HAVE AN ADVENTURE IN SCANDINAVIA

With the third largest population in Norway behind Oslo and Bergen, Trondheim is a cultural center. The Nidelva river runs through the center of the city and is lined with colorful, uniformly designed warehouses similar to those of Bryggen. The most recognizable architectural site in Trondheim is Nidaros Cathedral, a massive and ornate gothic cathedral built in the Middle Ages. The city is home to the Rockheim museum, with exhibits on the history of Norwegian rock music. By all accounts, it's a wonderful city to visit. Feel free to add it to your trip and choose your own adventure.

As for myself, all I saw of Trondheim was the mountainous locale from the airport window. Before I knew it, I was boarding another SAS airbus for the second part of my flight plan.

Getting situated, I noticed that my seat was a strange corner at the back of the plane with no window. As if seeing my plight, a male flight attendant approached.

"Do you really want to sit there?" he asked.

"This is what it says on my ticket," I replied.

"If you want a window," he motioned to the empty row across the aisle, "take a window."

Thanking him, I seated myself in an empty row with a nice view. It would be a good flight after all.

Like the crew of the *Fram*, I was about to venture beyond the limits of the day and night. The plane took off, and we moved over the Nordland region. Mountains and fjords passed below, the terrain becoming snowier.

At some point before the plane began a descent, we passed the Arctic Circle. This wasn't the final descent, but a brief stop in a smaller city in the northern part of the Nordland region.

Our stop in Bodø would be to refuel the plane for its final push to the northern tip of Norway. Descending through a thick cloud cover, very little was visible.

RAFFAEL CORONELLI

Clouds began to break and I got my first glimpse of the arctic landscape — jagged crags jutting up from the misty sea. What little I could see of Bodø already had a far different vibe — a smaller settlement wedged between giant rocks that loomed around it. This was a more naturally hostile environ that any I'd visited, into which the Nords had carved a small piece of civilization.

Plane refueled without having us disembark, it took off once more for the final push northward. Beyond the border of Nordland lay the county of Troms og Finnmark. The first part of its name came from the place I was going to spend the next two days.

Islands off the coast of Bodø

HOW TO HAVE AN ADVENTURE IN SCANDINAVIA

Beside rows of mountains icier and more extreme than those on the sides of the Sognefjord, on an island in the midst of a dark ocean, lay a city at the top of Norway.

Tromsø is the furthest north city on Earth with a population of over 70,000 people, its latitude higher than nearest contenders Norilsk and Murmansk (both in Russia). Even out the plane window, its hyperborean landscape was utterly unlike southern Norway.

Snow covered the ground in mid-May. The rugged arctic terrain with mountains dwarfing the city was far more alien than anything I'd seen further south. Tromsø is 217 miles north of the Arctic Circle, and it looked the part.

Tromsø's small airport didn't take long to navigate. I couldn't be bothered to figure out the bus, so I got a cab to the Hotel Enter Amelie at the city center.

The airport is on the opposite side of Tromsøya from the city center. Tromsøya is the island that makes up the main populated area, though the city also extends onto the mainland with the Tromsdalen neighborhood, and on the northern island Kvaløya in the opposite direction. I'd be visiting all three sections of the city during my visit.

Tromsø on approach by air

RAFFAEL CORONELLI

The cab ducked into a tunnel and took me to the other side of Tromsøya island. Streets lined with snow met us when we emerged, a suitably wintery scene for the Arctic. Tromsø doesn't get as much extreme weather as, say, Arctic Siberia, for the same reason that Norway has relatively hospitable temperatures — the Gulf Stream, bringing up air from further south across the Atlantic. By the time it reaches Norway's high north, however, it's still cold enough to leave snow on the ground in the month of May, preserving the otherworldly vibe of a place beyond the limits of time.

The cab dropped me off in front of the Hotel Enter Amelie. Check in wasn't available until 3:00PM, but they had a luggage room for me to store my bag for the day instead of lugging it around with me. Relieved of my bag, I headed back out to explore the Arctic city.

The hotel was a mere block from the waterfront. I stepped out onto the southeastern edge of Tromsøya, a cold sea breeze barreling down between the mountains and the ocean. Across the way was the mainland Tromsdalen area. Among the most prominent buildings in this mainland neighborhood, visible from the opposite shore, was the white, modern Arctic Cathedral.

The author of this book on the shore of Tromsøya (foreground)
Tromsdalen with the triangular Arctic Cathedral (background)

HOW TO HAVE AN ADVENTURE IN SCANDINAVIA

Behind that loomed Storsteinen, the mountain ledge to which the Fjellheisen cable car runs. I'd be taking that in the afternoon. Next to that at the south end of the valley stood Tromsdalstinden, considered to be a sacred mountain for the Sami. In Arctic Norway, Sami culture is far more prevalent than in the south, influencing traditions and cuisine. I'd get a taste of one of their dishes that afternoon.

A massive ship sat anchored next to the shore of Tromsøya where I walked. Bulky and utilitarian, the great metal hulk had the look of a ship that traversed the Arctic Ocean. Splotches across its surface told a story of frequent pummeling from hard weather.

RAFFAEL CORONELLI

There was something I wanted to check out nearby, on the block between the hotel and the edge of the island. It was an establishment that sounded cool by the name, but I was unprepared for what I was about to see.

In the second floor of a building by the Tromsøya waterfront is one of the best cultural museums in Norway, certainly the best I visited in Tromsø — the Troll Museum.

Opened in 2020, the Troll Museum is already notable for being the first of its kind in the region and has a wealth of in-depth, visually impressive exhibits on Norway's favorite folkloric creatures packed into its halls.

Climbing the stairs to the second story entrance, I encountered a group of kindergarten kids who'd been on a field trip to the museum. From the sound of their enthusiasm, they ate up what the museum had to offer — a good sign for any such establishment.

Admission at the front desk was about USD$18. The friendly curator explained the museum to me, including its use of augmented reality technology that you can access using tablets stationed throughout the exhibit halls.

The first case of augmented reality was a goofy, mirror-like panel allowing you to "see yourself as a troll" — placing the head of the museum's mascot, the Sea Troll, on your own body. AR technology came into play in a substantial way later on, but this was a fun way to begin.

Right:
The author of this book
as a Sea Troll

HOW TO HAVE AN ADVENTURE IN SCANDINAVIA

Entrance to the Troll Museum

A wall-mounted interactive map showed where different types of trolls lived in Norway. This comprehensive guide showcased geologic formations of interesting shapes and stories related to these creatures. Already, this was not a museum to speed through and see a few curiosities, but one with depth and immersion.

HOW TO HAVE AN ADVENTURE IN SCANDINAVIA

Further along the exhibit halls, installations showed fantastically designed statues and illustrations of Norway's various trolls and giants, from their origin with Norse mythology's Ymir to more recent additions to troll lore.

Left:
A diorama in the Troll Museum

A room dedicated to *Peer Gynt* showcased a diorama of the scene scored by Grieg's "In the Hall of the Mountain King", its display perfectly supplementing my visit to Troldhaugen the day before. The augmented reality tablet on hand added movement and effects to the mesmerizing diorama.

Right:
A sign for a troll-only staff room

193

One area of the exhibit hall focused on sea creatures, including a full-scale statue of a creature I'd never heard of before, but was prominently featured in the museum's imagery — the Sea Troll. The figure looked fairly lifelike and had an impressive level of detail.

Across from the Sea Troll stood a woman with blazing red-dyed hair, in a Troll Museum staff T-shirt.

"Is this an original character?" I asked.

She replied that he was, and is the museum's contribution to local lore. Tromsø itself is unfortunately not tied to any troll-related legends despite being the location of the museum, prompting them to create one. The Sea Troll is popular with children, and functions as a local mascot. Its amphibiousness ties to Tromsø's role as an Arctic fishing port with some of the most delicious seafood in Europe.

This woman's name was Tonje Sommerli, a teacher at the Troll Museum. She'd been the one educating the kindergartners I'd seen on the way in. She's also a writer, and told me of a historical fiction book she was writing about the 16th century period during which Denmark controlled Norway. Keep an eye out for it when it's published! I told her of my frustration that Tromso wasn't mentioned in any English-language guidebooks I'd looked at, but that I'd be prominently mentioning the fantastic Troll Museum in my own travel book.

I asked about actual folklore of the arctic region. Extremely knowledgeable, she told me of how the medieval Nords considered the arctic to be the realm of black magic. A 16th century cardinal even claimed Arctic Norway to be the location of the entrance to the afterlife.

As she relayed to me, arctic Norway was historically a penal colony, a place where witches were persecuted, and a land too far away for the Danish to bother sending their emissaries. This all allowed the Troms og Finnmark region to develop its own unique cultural identity.

HOW TO HAVE AN ADVENTURE IN SCANDINAVIA

The Sea Troll

RAFFAEL CORONELLI

Old Man of the Forest diorama at the Troll Museum

HOW TO HAVE AN ADVENTURE IN SCANDINAVIA

She asked of my plans for the city, and I said I was taking a guided fjord tour the next day, but that the booking came with a warning that it might be canceled.

"If it does get canceled," she said, "take the bus out to Kvaløya."

A bus ticket, she informed me, is infinitely cheaper than a guided tour, and walking around Kvaløya would allow me to see everything. Kvaløya also has reindeer who roam around and occasionally come up onto the road. This option would indeed be much cheaper than the tour, so I kept it in my potential itinerary.

Post-Troll Museum that afternoon, my plans were the Polar Museum and the Fjellheisen cable car. She described the Polar Museum as a "hunting museum," and that I should go up in the cable car before 3:00PM to avoid it getting too packed with tourists who stop in Tromsø on a cruise ship for the afternoon. This nixed the Polar Museum from my schedule, as it closed at 5. I'd end up getting a chance to see it the following day, anyhow.

I asked her about local food, and she told me to try reindeer stew — a Sami delicacy. Tonje also gave me a recommendation for the best seafood in the city — Arctandria, a phenomenal suggestion for the next evening.

Thanking Tonje again for letting me bother her for roughly an hour, I bought a Sea Troll magnet from the gift shop. This and other trinkets function with augmented reality like the museum's exhibits, viewable using the Troll Museum app.

I can't recommend the Troll Museum highly enough if you're visiting Tromsø. For someone whose interest in Norwegian folklore and its bestiaries partially drew me to the country in the first place, it ended up being one of the best museums in Norway that I was able to see.

On the way out, I messaged my friend Alex Gayhart (who drew the illustration of the Kraken that appears on the front cover and in full later in the book) telling him that I'd gone to a Troll Museum, along with a few photos.

"That's absolutely the best thing," he messaged back. *"If I went on the trip, this would be what I went on about."*

With that, I headed out to catch the bus over to Fjellheisen. I had to take Tonje's advice and get there before the busy hours.

On the way to the bus stop, I made note of a weirdly common theme in Tromsø. There are lots of public statues of nude figures, both male and female, throughout the city in random places. I wonder if arctic people long to be free of their heavy clothes and bask in the sun — a longing that cannot be fulfilled, as dictated by the harshness of the region's weather. This is my personal psycho-sociological theory and has no evidence to support it.

The most bang for your buck you can get on public transportation in Tromsø is a 24-hour bus pass. Unfortunately, the app for their transit system is extremely confusing, so it's much easier to buy a ticket at a bus ticket vending machine like the one I used at the Fr. Langes Gt. stop just a few blocks from the Troll Museum. From there, I walked another few blocks to the Kystens Hus bus stop in time to catch the 26 bus across the bridge to Fjellheisen.

The Tromsøbrua cantilevered bridge raised the bus high over the icy waters. On the oncoming shore, the mainland Tromsdalen neighborhood waited. Above it towered the mountain up which I'd be taking the cable car.

Unlike Fløyen in Bergen, this mountain was covered in snow and ice, even more so than the mountain I'd climbed in Balestrand. There would be little chance of a hike around the top level. The observation deck and restaurant at the top would have to be sufficient entertainment for the afternoon.

HOW TO HAVE AN ADVENTURE IN SCANDINAVIA

The bus dropped me off in the midst of a residential area. As one of Tromsø's biggest tourist attractions, the low-key setting of Fjellheisen's lower station is emblematic of the city's out-of-the-way charm. This wasn't like Bergen's theme park entrance to the Floibanen station. Fjellheisen's station was a small wooden house on a quiet residential street with some cables sticking out of the back of it and extending up the majestic, icy rock face.

The cable car leaves on the half hour. Make sure you don't miss the car, as you'll be stranded for another half hour if you do. I had fifteen minutes to kill, and the station house is fairly tiny, so I was open to suggestions.

"Is there something to do around here while I wait?" I asked the lady at the ticket counter.

"Not really," she said. "You can walk around the neighborhood and see what it looks like."

I laughed at the mundanity of her suggestion. Norwegians are nothing if not frank and to-the-point. With that as my option, I took a stroll up and down the street until it was almost time to depart. The houses were average-sized and seemed well kept up. It might be a nice neighborhood in which to live, I thought, so long as too many tourists don't wander through your front yard while waiting for the cable car.

Time almost up, I headed back and waited by the car until the gate opened. Only two other tourists boarded with me. If there was to be a big rush, I'd missed it with Tonje's advice. Then, with a lurch, we were off.

Unlike a funicular, the Fjellheisen cable car hangs in the air from its cables. This immediately gave the impression of soaring over the Arctic landscape, pulling back from the city as we ascended. Snowy rocks and crags passed beneath the cable car, the quiet rumble of the motor the only sound. It was like flying over an alien world.

RAFFAEL CORONELLI

Tromsø from the top of Fjellheisen

Pulling into the top station at the Storsteinen ledge, I exited the platform through a rustic wooden door and found myself in the enclosed station and visitor center. A door opened to the ledge outside, so I pulled it open and stepped out into an icy blast of mountain wind.

Snow covered the ledge except for the observation deck, which had been cleared away. I stepped up to the railing. Just below at the foot of the mountain, the Tromsdalen neighborhood was barely visible. Tromsøya island, where I was staying, was entirely within view. Beyond that were the outer fjords of Kvaløya island, the place Tonje had recommended me to go the following day.

The elevation and the latitude combined to make this place's extremity feel far more heightened than anywhere else I'd been. Icy blue was the primary color of my entire field of vision, a sun that would not set peering down through a cloud layer that I was at least partially above. Tromsø, the Norwegian Arctic, was a cold world away from anywhere else.

Behind the station and the observation deck, a great field of snow extended across the mountain ledge. This was impassable without snow gear, but I climbed atop the snow drift and tried to walk around for a brief moment anyway.

HOW TO HAVE AN ADVENTURE IN SCANDINAVIA

Storsteinen ledge

As I'd suspected, the elements made it impossible to go on a full hike. Luckily, the station at Storsteinen ledge is homey, welcoming, and at the time, uncrowded. I stepped back inside and made a B-line for the Fjellstua Cafe.

For a place that gave such an impression of being a remote, out of the way outpost, the Storsteinen station had an excellent dining facility. The traditional regional food at the counter-serve cafe and bar was one of the more worthwhile things to experience at the mountaintop.

The menu included a variety of traditional North Norwegian dishes. Since it was still the afternoon and I didn't expect to be at the top of Storsteinen for long, little did I know, I skipped food and ordered a Mack Pilsner. Mack bills itself as the "World's Northernmost Brewery," which may well be accurate, as it makes its beer more than 200 miles north of the Arctic Circle. It was a fine Pilsner, made all the more interesting by the view. High up over Tromsø, I enjoyed my drink in a realm of clouds and ice.

Finished with a couple of minutes to spare before the cable car left. I packed up and headed down to the launch chamber from where to the car docked. I swiped my return ticket at the gate — only to find the platform empty. The cable car had left, even though there was still a minute to spare before the top of the hour.

RAFFAEL CORONELLI

"It left without you," said the operator, coming up to me with an apologetic look. "If no one's here, we just send it down."

It could've waited until it was fully time to go, but there was nothing to be done. The operator explained that he'd let me through when the next car arrived in another half hour, since I'd used up my return ticket getting onto the empty platform.

Stranded on Storsteinen ledge over a thousand feet above Tromsø, I returned to the restaurant and decided there was only one thing left to do. It was time for dinner.

Among the menu options, there was one that stood out to me the most. Reindeer stew — one of Tonje's recommendations for local food — is a Sami home-cooked specialty, a hearty food of the reindeer herders of Scandinavia's Arctic regions. I loved the reindeer sausage I'd had in Bergen. The reindeer meat served at Storsteinen station is locally sourced in Sørreisa, just a bit south of Tromsø, and the stew is served with mushrooms, potatoes, and lingonberries — foods of Arctic Norway.

Having placed my order at the counter, I turned around to see a woman sitting in the spot where I'd been sitting. I thought nothing of it, and prepared to sit at the next table over.

Left:
A Mack pilsner
at the Fjellstua Cafe

HOW TO HAVE AN ADVENTURE IN SCANDINAVIA

"Sorry," she said in an American accent, "I took your spot!"

"That's fine!" I laughed.

This funny introduction lead to a conversation, spurring me to sit across from her. Shortly, her colleagues returned from outside — and things got interesting.

One of the men was the U.S. Coordinator for the Arctic Region. The woman with whom I'd been talking, Hilary, was his senior adviser. All were members of the United States State Department, and were in Tromsø to attend an international conference on security in the arctic regions. They were a trio of interesting people, but more than that, they were involved in the workings of international affairs at a time and in a place where things were in a state of historic tension.

It was May of 2022. Just over two months prior, Russia had launched their brutal invasion of Ukraine. Russia shares a short northeastern border with Norway's Finnmark region at the top of the Arctic, as well as a long border with Finland. That very week, both Sweden and Finland had applied to be part of NATO (an organization to which both Norway and Denmark already belonged) in response to their neighbor's shocking attack on Ukraine.

As they explained while understandably declining to give specifics, there was one country in particular that controlled a lot of real estate in the Arctic, and had recently violated the trust of others in the region. This had been a major topic of conversation at the conference, which included officials from countries the world over.

Here I was, in Norway's high north, talking to U.S. government officials involved in international diplomacy at a time when tensions in the region were at an alarming high. On the opposite side of the planet, it can be difficult to rationalize what it's like when a country next door starts invading their neighbors. Norway was full of Ukrainian flags and support for that country and its populace.

RAFFAEL CORONELLI

Reindeer Stew at Fjellstua Cafe

In the midst of our conversation, my reindeer stew was ready. Retrieving it at the counter, I hurried back to continue the scintillating chat and dig in. Tonje had been right — the stew was hearty, delicious, and exactly what my tired self needed after not having eaten since breakfast.

HOW TO HAVE AN ADVENTURE IN SCANDINAVIA

The conversation wasn't all doom and gloom and international tensions. These three liked traveling in Norway, and were enjoying their reindeer burgers as much as I was enjoying my reindeer stew. That all three U.S. government officials got burgers for dinner was somewhat amusing — albeit made with local ingredients.

It was certainly interesting to run into foreign policy professionals operating at such a tense moment for the high north. I asked the State Department officials as I was leaving how much trouble I'd get in if I mentioned them in the book I was writing. They said none, so we'll see what happens. They weren't the last people with a connection to the international situation I'd encounter in Tromsø.

Saying our goodbyes, I left them to their discussions and headed down to the cable car. The operator let me through, as he'd promised. With a jerking motion and a whirl of servos, the car moved down the cables, swooping across the mountainside. In such vast nature, I considered my place in all of it. Such a conversation was a reminder of the tumultuous world in which we live.

View from the Fjellheisen cable car

A few blocks down the road, I caught the bus at the Novasenteret stop. Rumbling across the bridge, I returned to the island, and soon was back at the hotel. I'd been gone the whole day and still had yet to check in, so I took care of that with the help of the Enter Amelie Hotel's friendly desk clerk. Bag collected from the luggage room, I headed up.

Tromsø experiences full 24-hour day from the end of May through August. In mid-May, the time of my visit, it was very nearly there. In fact, the sun doesn't completely set, just dips a little bit and then goes back up. Choosing a time to visit depends on whether you want to see the midnight sun, or the northern lights. Either way, you're in for a strange daylight schedule.

The city spawned a handful of notable low-key, ambient electronic music artists in the 90s and 2000s, including Röyksopp. That vibe feels inspired by the quiet sense of suspended animation one experiences in a time of day that doesn't change.

I'd had a long day, having traversed most of the north-south length of Norway. I'd met trolls and the experts who study them, and people from the U.S. government involved in international diplomacy. If I wanted to do anything the next day, I needed to get some sleep.

I closed the blackout curtains. The midnight sun would have to wait for tomorrow.

Exploring Tromsø and Kvaløya:
The Top of the World

Sure enough, a last-minute email told me that my fjord tour was canceled. "Weather" was cited as being the reason for it, but the weather forecast in Tromsø that day was hardly terrible. Whatever the reason, the guides left me in the lurch, at least granting me a refund. Luckily, Tonje's recommendations left me with more options, particularly a plan to go out to the island of Kvaløya to the north and see some of the arctic wilds for myself.

Upon opening the blackout curtain at 6:00 AM, the sun was just as high in the sky as it had been when I'd gone to sleep. I showered and dressed for the arctic with a thermal undershirt and down coat (the region is cold in May even in spite of the Gulf Stream).

Breakfast at the Enter Amelie was another Nordic buffet; not as extensive as Scandic's, but with the pickled herring and locks standards and plenty of continental options. They also had to-go cups for the coffee, which I used to bring one with me for the road.

I made a brief stop at the Roald Amundsen monument in a square just blocks from the hotel. Amundsen is an arctic hero for reasons discussed in the *Fram* section, that ship itself having launched from Tromsø on its voyage north.

RAFFAEL CORONELLI

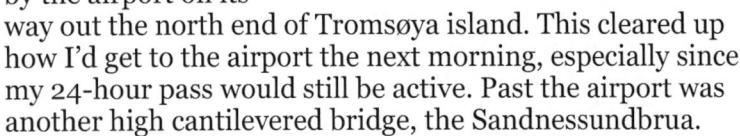

**Right:
Roald Amundsen
monument**

I, too, would be going north that day — not to the pole like Amundsen, but the furthest I'd ever been.

The real first order of business was getting a new bus pass. I once again purchased that at the Fr. Langes Gt. stop and returned to the bus stop just across from the hotel to catch the 42 bus.

The 42 has a stop by the airport on its way out the north end of Tromsøya island. This cleared up how I'd get to the airport the next morning, especially since my 24-hour pass would still be active. Past the airport was another high cantilevered bridge, the Sandnessundbrua.

This bridge is the only means by which the main part of Tromsø is connected to Kvaløya island. I wondered if the Sea Troll was lurking in the waves beneath it.

Sandnessundbrua bridge to Kvaløya

HOW TO HAVE AN ADVENTURE IN SCANDINAVIA

Kvaløya

From my first glimpses, Kvaløya was mountainous, rugged, and more wild than Tromsøya. The Kvaløysletta neighborhood is the first settlement just over the bridge, occupying a strip of land along the shoreline that faces the north side of the southern island. Beyond, the bus moved along a shoreline road with sparser buildings.

Just inland was a towering row of mountains, the same ones I'd seen from the Storsteinen overlook across the city. I wouldn't be climbing these, but even traveling around their base felt like a remote experience.

My advice had been to go to the end of the bus route and walk from there toward the Kaldfjord — one of the great fjords in Kvaløya. I got off at the end of the line, Eikjosen, just inland from the bay that shares its name.

The bus turned around and left, leaving me alone in a cold landscape. Wind blew a light flurry against me, so I donned my poncho to keep myself dry and began my walk.

Only a few kilometers north of the city, this stretch of Kvaløya had a far more remote vibe than even Storsteinen. That had the visitor center and an easy access to the cable car down the mountain. The further I walked from the bus stop, the deeper I submerged into the height of the northern wilds.

Snow and ice clung to the slopes on either side, open fields of frost accompanying my walk on the roadside footpath. The ravine through which I crossed cut through the middle of the island's mountains on a stretch of land at the end of a fjord.

Tour be damned, I'd spent a mere ten dollars on a bus pass and gotten myself to a place where I could see at least one of the fjords.

A tour might be preferable for anyone who doesn't want to walk around by themselves all day. For myself, the solitude was part of the experience. I was on a northern arctic island amidst vast nature, enveloped in its majesty. To get anywhere — back to the bus stop, or forward to the next town — I had to journey across frozen landscapes.

The gap between the mountains opened ahead to the tip of a sharp blade of ocean waves rimmed by a small town. It was the Kaldfjord — literally "cold fjord." I'm sure one could try to find a colder fjord, but I don't know how successful the search would be. Kaldfjord was a sheer arctic gash into the center of Kvaløya from the opposite side.

Moving into the quaint town at the fjordside, I felt that I'd reached an extremity of the Earth. Past the waters of Kaldfjorden lay only the polar regions to which the Fram had journeyed. Children from a local school walked by, the only residents out and about.

The cold north waves stretched from my right side. On the left, to the west as I continued up the coast, arose a wintry slope. Low hanging clouds added to the mythic vibe of the place, putting the epic vista in a hazy filter like a scene from a legend.

Kvaløya sits at a crossroad between oceans. To the north, the Barents Sea churns northward into the Arctic Ocean. To the west, the Norwegian Sea connects to the North Atlantic. Kaldfjord's waters mix both in its freezing cauldron between the mountains.

HOW TO HAVE AN ADVENTURE IN SCANDINAVIA

Kaldfjord

Somewhere on this island were herds of reindeer. They remained hidden, but I was enjoying the environ enough whether or not they showed themselves.

A spot next to the road extended off onto a small dock. Private fishing boats sat moored in the water. It was a perfect vantage point from which to see Henrikvika Bay, the point at which the Kaldfjord turns a corner and continues out to the sea. Just past the bend stood Store Blåmann, Kvaløya's tallest mountain. I might've been in someone's way if they'd come to unmoor their boat, but I was alone. I watched the drifting waters and the breathed in the misty, frigid air. This beautiful locale was all one could ask for in an arctic vista.

Having enjoyed Kaldfjorden and walked a good deal of the way along its shore, I decided it was time to turn back. It would've made sense for reindeer to roam around more inland. The fjord's sheer mountainsides made it impossible to get too far away from the main road. I'd look for a place where I might be able to walk around the terrain a bit more.

Passing through the town once more, I bid a silent farewell to the arctic fjord. I continued up the road until I'd passed the bus stop where I'd been dropped off. Even closer to Tromsø proper by a negligible amount, Kvaløya didn't lose any of its remote charm.

On the opposite side of the stretch of land cut away by the Kaldfjord is another bay, Eidkjosen. This place faces out toward Tromsøya island from about fifteen kilometers away. Small roadside businesses popped up periodically. On the other side of the street was a residential district with houses. A man who likely lived nearby walked his dog up the road.

A number of roadside shacks stood periodically by the water. I'm not sure what purpose they served, but they provided rustic pieces of set dressing that fit the vibe.

HOW TO HAVE AN ADVENTURE IN SCANDINAVIA

A shack on Kvaløya

All the while, I kept on the lookout for a path inland, or a park of some kind. I wanted to get to a place where reindeer could, if not be seen, then at least could have congregated. The road was unbelievably scenic, but I wanted to fully immerse in nature as much as one can when snow covers the ground and hiking boots don't cut it.

My search led me to a road up through a residential area. Briefly getting phone reception, I noticed a nearby spot on the map that might fit my desired destination — Storelva Skistadion. The name literally means "ski stadium," but it's more of a public park where cross-country skiing events are sometimes held.

RAFFAEL CORONELLI

Storelva Skistadion

Climbing up the narrow road past residential houses, I found myself at a single remote two-story building in the middle of a vast field of snow against the backdrop of the majestic Rødtind mountain. Something about the scene gave off the vibe of the abandoned Norwegian Antarctic research station in *The Thing*, a thought that amused me somewhat. From what I can gather, the building houses offices related to the park's skiing events with, to my knowledge, no aliens running amok.

The Skistadion park was empty, all the way up to the slopes of Rødtind. If I could see anything related to the presence of reindeer on this island, this was it.

Snow is not the easiest thing to walk in, especially when it's up to your shins and you've pulled a ligament in your knee a week prior. The elements were harsh, but then why come to the Arctic if I didn't want to deal with them?

Trudging through the snow, I climbed atop a small protruding boulder to get better footing. From atop the boulder, I surveyed frozen field all around. The Rødtind peak hung overhead.

HOW TO HAVE AN ADVENTURE IN SCANDINAVIA

The wilds of Kvaløya

RAFFAEL CORONELLI

Reindeer tracks on Kvaløya

HOW TO HAVE AN ADVENTURE IN SCANDINAVIA

It was then that I noticed patterns in the snow before me, extending into the distance. They were tracks, and they were big — hoof prints larger than those of a normal deer. There could only have been one animal that made them.

Reindeer live across multiple continents in the polar region, having migrated across the ice cap. They've been in the Norwegian Arctic since before the arrival of humans, and are intrinsically part of the Sami cultural identity. I'd eaten those farmed by reindeer herders in stews and sausages. Here, I was looking at the tracks of a wild one.

Though I would've liked to, the fact that I didn't see the live reindeer who made those tracks added something to the mystique. They were made by an elusive, almost mystical creature that didn't want to be disturbed.

Reindeer tracks before me in the white snow, I stood with my weatherproof outfit flapping in the wind. It was another moment of sublimity on this island that was the furthest north I'd go. My journey had taken me here, to this hyperborean place at the top of the world.

I made a note to remember that feeling. It was why I'd come to the Arctic.

The author of this book on Kvaløya

With that, I stepped off the rock and trudged back through the snow in the opposite direction of the reindeer's tracks, my hiking boots leaving far less graceful marks in the surface. The reindeer had gone inland to its mountain home, myself back to the road to catch the bus to Tromsø.

The 42 bus picked me up at the roadside, and soon I was rumbling over the Sandnessundbrua bridge to Tromsøya island. The magic of Kvaløya still played in my mind, but it wasn't as if the place I was in was any less spectacular — I still had much of Tromsø to explore through the afternoon.

I disembarked at the city center and headed to a place that had been on the agenda the previous day — the Polar Museum. I didn't know what to expect from it after Tonje had described it as a "hunting museum", but it still sounded like something to check out.

Getting there was easy; in fact, getting anywhere in Tromsø is far easier than in other Norwegian cities I'd tried to navigate. The street plan is close to a grid, and the short distances on Tromsøya make it highly walkable. Who'd have thought that the most easily navigable city I visited in Norway would've been the one 217 miles north of the Arctic Circle?

Across the street from the 19th Century warehouse building that houses the Polar Museum, I saw two familiar faces — Tonje and the Troll Museum's curator. Naturally, I walked over and said hello, obnoxiously interrupting their task of scouting out an augmented reality walking tour of Tromsø based on Sami folklore. The tour would be the first of its kind, the curator proudly informed me, another feat for the high-tech and forward-thinking museum of Norway's mythological past.

Turning my attention to the Polar Museum, I paid the roughly USD$10 ticket price and was handed an English-language pamphlet to translate the Norwegian text in the exhibits.

HOW TO HAVE AN ADVENTURE IN SCANDINAVIA

Polar Museum in Tromsø with a docked cruise ship in the background

Having opened in the 1970s, the Polar Museum is an extensive taxidermy and artifact collection that tells about the animals of the region and the life of early explorers who struggled to survive alongside them. It gave lots of information and had an old fashioned museum vibe.

The Polar Museum is owned and operated by the Arctic University of Norway, UiT. They operate another museum on the south end of Tromsøya called the Arctic University Museum, to which I did not get. This newer museum has exhibits about Sami culture and scientific subjects relating to the Arctic region.

Post-Polarmuseet, I returned to the outside world to find it far more crowded. This was because, as I'd been warned the day before, a cruise ship had docked at the port. Cruise ships bring tourists up to Tromsø, let them wander around for an afternoon, then load them back up and leave.

A few blocks south of the Polarmuseet was Kystens Hus, a large building dedicated to the offices of arctic fishing companies. It advertises itself like a museum, but upon entering to check it out sans-admission, I found its exhibits to essentially be promotional installations for the fishing industry.

RAFFAEL CORONELLI

It was still interesting to see the headquarters from where arctic fishing operations are orchestrated ahead of my arctic seafood dinner. Kystens Hus contains several seafood restaurants itself, getting their food straight from the source, including a high-end sushi bar that I'm sure is delicious with the level of fish on hand. I'd be holding out for Arctandria, but if you have more dinners in Tromsø, I'd imagine the restaurants here are worth checking out.

A fun-looking option for lunch is located a few blocks inland by the square that houses the statue of King Haakon. Raketten Bar & Pølse is an outdoor sausage stand stand that serves alcohol and bills itself as "The Tiniest Bar in the Universe." Whether this statement is technically accurate is irrelevant; the pointy-roofed hut looks the part enough to get away with it.

Right:
Raketten
Bar & Pølse

HOW TO HAVE AN ADVENTURE IN SCANDINAVIA

One other Tromsø fixture I didn't get a chance to check out for myself is Bastard Bar, a bar and music venue with a cheeky English name located in the heart of the city center. Tonje had mentioned it in her rundown of the city's hotspots, but there weren't any shows while I was in town.

I did see that Bizarrekult, a recent favorite of mine whose album *Vi Overlevde* (Norwegian for "We Survived") saw heavy rotation from me on trains and flights during the trip, played Bastard Bar a few weeks after my trip. Fronted by an ex-Siberian who expatriated to slightly less frostbitten Oslo to live the Black Metal dream, the icy and atmospheric Bizarrekult would've been the perfect band to have seen in the Arctic.

I made a quick stop back at the hotel to freshen up. My long walk through the arctic elements on Kvaløya had left me looking somewhat disheveled, a state in which I couldn't visit a high end restaurant. After a shower and a change of clothes, I headed south toward the place I'd been told was the best seafood restaurant in Tromsø.

Past the Amundsen monument, past the oceanfront hotels and around the corner was an unassuming building containing two high-end restaurants. On the ground floor was a steakhouse, not something associated with Norwegian cuisine. Climbing the staircase to the second floor, seafaring-related decorations greeted me along the walls before I even got to the entrance.

Once in the door, the charming seafaring theme let me know exactly what type of restaurant I was in for. Arctandria's front window overlooks Tromsø's harbor with the majestic, snowy fjord in the background. I was seated in view of it by an enthusiastic waitress who promptly asked me what I'd like to drink.

"What Norwegian aquavits do you have?" I asked, my stock response at this point in the trip.

RAFFAEL CORONELLI

The waitress offered to bring me her personal recommendation, which I of course welcomed. It was a smaller brand called Maquavit. I'm not sure what the name implies, but it was a rich, well-aged caramel color after maturing for five years. Promotional material calls it Northern Norway's own Aquavit; since I had it by recommendation of an arctic native, it must be! It was delicious, and was a great primer for the meal.

My first course was a tomato and seafood soup. It was exquisite, a perfectly blended combination of flavors. The waitress paired it and my entree with a Riesling after I'd finished my aquavit. I'm normally not big on Riesling, but this was a fine pairing with the opulent appetizer.

I was okay with this meal costing a little more, too. My canceled tour had been refunded, enlarging the trip budget.

My entree, three arctic fillets and some invertebrates, was decadent. It consisted of arctic char, salmon, and halibut, all three of which were caught locally in the freezing waters off Tromsø. Shrimp and mussels rounded out the dish, and all were served over a risotto.

Arctandria was indeed one of the best seafood restaurants to which I've ever been. The atmospheric decor, the professionalism and knowledge of the servers, and most importantly, the unbelievably good, fresh arctic seafood made my trip to the region feel complete. The service had been impeccable and greatly added to my enjoyment of the meal, the suggested pairings enhancing the already excellent food. Tromsø has a lot to offer, but its unique placement in the topmost region of Norway makes a seafood restaurant like Arctandria unsurpassable.

I remembered as I headed outside into an evening as bright as noon that I'd missed midnight the night before. I wouldn't make that mistake again. To bide the time, I'd go grab a drink at one last recommended establishment.

HOW TO HAVE AN ADVENTURE IN SCANDINAVIA

Right:
Arctandria
seafood soup

Left:
Three arctic
fillets at
Arctandria

RAFFAEL CORONELLI

Ølhallen

HOW TO HAVE AN ADVENTURE IN SCANDINAVIA

Ølhallen, literally "the beer hall," was a short walk inland on Storgata. "Tromsøs eldeste pub," read the sign on the old world storefront with a wooden door, a setup from when Ølhallen opened in 1928.

Upon entering, the old world vibe only increased. A taxidermy polar reared up in a silent roar near the bar area. 72 beers were on tap at the bar, according to their website, and the line of taps certainly looked it. The Mack microbrewery (the beer I had atop Storsteinen) is next door, and their entire lineup is prominently displayed. It was all a bit overwhelming.

"Are these all from Norway?" I asked the bar tender.

On the other side of the bar was a young woman with magazine-cover looks and long, light brown hair flowing from under a beanie hat. Her fashion sense struck a balance between arctic snowboarder and urban bohemian. She explained that the beers were indeed Norwegian, coming from across the country. I asked for her recommendations with the note that I like darker beers, but can generally enjoy anything.

I pointed out a "licorice stout."

"That's for if you like licorice beers..." she warned me, something that didn't sound terribly appealing.

With Vlada's (the bartender's) expert guidance, I was able to use my better judgment and ended up with a solid Norwegian porter. After, I asked for her favorite Mack beer.

Through all of this between orders, I got to talking to Vlada. We discussed my trip, how it was my last night in Tromsø, and how the next day I'd be off to Denmark.

"You're on a Scandinavia trip?" she inferred.

I told her about how I'd chosen Scandinavia out of all the possible destinations for my first big trip since the pandemic, how it'd been at the top of the list. She agreed, being a world traveler herself and having moved to Norway in 2019 after living a few different places.

I asked where she was from originally.

"Ukraine," she replied.

Immediately, my brain drew connections to recent events, and things became more serious.

"Oh, wow," I said, unsure of how to proceed with the big questions. "Do you have family there?"

She told me how she was able to get her parents out when the invasion occurred and bring them to Norway. I was relieved to hear it. Her brother, though, was still there. Men around our age weren't allowed to leave Ukraine due to the war, meaning he had to remain in the country.

Her eyes drifted away for a moment, attention understandably elsewhere.

I asked if he was fighting. She said no, and that she hoped it wouldn't come to that. I agreed.

World events that are continents away can seem distant, even if you get a visceral shock from them happening. When you're talking to someone so directly effected, your degree of separation shrinks to nothing.

Vlada was holding it together on a heroic level, all things considered. In the face of all of it, she was helping her family and thriving in Norway.

I told her about my encounter with the US State Department officials. We talked about the arctic security conference, which she knew about.

"There's not much we can do besides support," she said.

We both hoped the conflict would end soon.

Eventually, the conversation turned back to the less severe. She apologized for the weather, but I said I'd enjoyed it anyway. When the midnight sun is out with a clear sky, she told me, it's beautiful.

She then revealed that she was a snowboarder. I'd called it based on her overall look.

"I was gonna say," I laughed, "you look like a snowboarder."

HOW TO HAVE AN ADVENTURE IN SCANDINAVIA

Interior of Ølhallen

She found that amusing. Tromsø is an ideal place for snow sports, as evidenced by the ski course I'd walked through on Kvaløya earlier in the day.

I told her I was writing a book about the trip, to which she showed interest. We exchanged instagram handles to keep in touch after the trip while I worked on it and published it.

I was glad to have met someone so interesting on my final night in Tromsø. What had started as a brief excursion to a bar had become an important and enriching human interaction, one that made the world feel more connected at a time when that was sorely needed. Beyond sightseeing and checklists, this is what I get from traveling — the real adventure.

Three beers deep and with more customers coming in for Vlada to take care of, I closed out and bid farewell to my new friend.

Outside, the sky had cleared up. The sun shone bright as if it were mid afternoon at 8:04 PM.

Clouds returned as the night progressed. By 10:00 PM, the sun peeked through a misty overcast sky, just as it had on Kvaløya that morning.

Around 11:50 PM, a brief dusk fell as the sun dipped a bit toward the horizon. It wasn't the blazing high noon of a month later, but it wouldn't fully set.

At midnight, the sky over Tromsø was a deep blue like the waters of the Arctic sea.

Tromsø at night in mid-May

The Pearl Seaways docked at Bjørvika in Oslo

Leaving Norway:
A Ship on the Oslofjord

As I awoke, the never-setting sun broke through the clouds and bathed the city. Among other things, it made me wish I had one more day in arctic Norway.

That wasn't the plan, though. I had a boat to catch.

After wolfing down one last Norwegian buffet breakfast next to my luggage, I checked out and crossed the street to the bus stop. The bus traversed the island of Tromsøya north, along the same route that had brought me to Kvaløya the day before. I half wanted to stay on the bus — keep going to Kvaløya — maybe see a reindeer.

Tromsø is like a place from a dream, a liminal zone where the laws of reality don't hold as fast as elsewhere. This was the one stop on the trip that I felt could've used an extra day. It wasn't the attractions or activities, but the place itself. As I boarded the direct flight south to Oslo and sat next to my window, I took one last look out at a place that was unlike any other.

The clear sky beckoned. Snowy mountains reflected the sun from beneath. Tromsø had found its way into my heart like a glacier carving a fjord into a mountain range.

The city pulled away beneath. Troms' hyperborean landscape rolled under the plane, turning to rows of fjords, and then to the landscape of central and southern Norway.

RAFFAEL CORONELLI

A sense of deja vu struck me as I navigated Oslo Airport and boarded the express train to the Sentralstasjon. My time in Norway was ending with a coda, a once-foreign experience now familiar. Knowing exactly where to go, I exited the station on the south end by the Opera House.

On the harbor, moored at the shore of the Oslofjord, was a great ship. Its side decal read "DFDS," its operating line. The expanse of its multi-level deck was visible from over a kilometer away. It was the *Pearl Seaways*, a massive ferry that would facilitate my overnight journey to Denmark.

Despite being visible clear across the Bjørvika bay due to the ship's immense size, the DFDS terminal was a bit of a walk to get to. Crossing Oslo's waterfront, I traced my steps in reverse from the first full day in Norway when I walked to the Opera House from Akershus Fortress.

Before entering the terminal, situated near the fortress, I stood next to the immense ship. Its metal hull eclipsed the city behind it. Machines clanked and whirred as they loaded supply containers into the hold through the open back where passenger cars would drive in.

Inside the terminal, I tried checking in at one of the self-service machines. It didn't want to read my passport for some reason, so I had to check in at the manned desk with the help of an actual human being. That worked much more smoothly, as it usually does in such a scenario. Boarding wasn't to begin until 2:45, so I had a bit of time to kill before I could go on the ship. I decided to take the opportunity to go inland and take one more walk around Oslo.

Something I wanted to bring back with me from Norway was a bottle of Norwegian aquavit. I'd sampled a few and liked them all, so I would've been fine with buying any of them. I just had to find where to look for one.

HOW TO HAVE AN ADVENTURE IN SCANDINAVIA

With this vague idea in mind, I walked across the Akershus Fortress grounds and up Kongens gate. The now-familiar city greeted me. I don't know if I'd missed Oslo, per se, but it felt welcoming coming back after a week and a half galavanting through the Norwegian wilds. The streets had their chaotic energy, the people walking as fast as ever.

What didn't get any easier was navigation. Soon enough, I had no idea where I was. I knew I'd headed in the complete wrong direction when I found myself back at the familiar sight of Oslo Cathedral, the street-disrupting edifice located at a crossroads a bit of a way inland.

For one last time in my trip, I was lost in Oslo. My search for a souvenir aquavit was canceled. I now had to find the waterfront. Turning and twisting around a few more streets in the opposite direction of the cathedral, I spotted the dual brown brick towers of Rådhuset over the tops of buildings. That gave me some bearings, pointing the way to the water.

Before long, I was back at Akershus Fortress with no souvenir but one last directionally confounding Oslo experience. I almost cherished the frustration. It wouldn't be Oslo without it.

Just before heading back to the ship, I stopped into a Joker convenience store to buy toothpaste. Joker is one of the more common convenience store chains in Norway. Despite not finding my aquavit in Oslo, I did find some toothpaste with Norwegian writing on the tube. You take what you can get sometimes.

One last time, I passed Akershus. The castle wall fell away and revealed the Pearl Seaways waiting at the dock.

Inside the terminal, the gate had opened. A ticket officer checked my passport and ticket and let me pass. Customs wasn't necessary at any point, since both Norway and Denmark are in the Schengen Zone.

RAFFAEL CORONELLI

Boarding the Pearl Seaways in Oslo

HOW TO HAVE AN ADVENTURE IN SCANDINAVIA

I rode the escalator to the second level and stepped out onto the enclosed boarding bridge. Through the glass, I peered down the length of the hull from midship. It was a massive vessel, which would give me plenty to explore on the 17-hour journey. It felt a bit like boarding the *Titanic*, though hopefully without the events of that voyage. There were other things to watch out for in the Kattegat.

The entrance hall on deck five led me to a row of elevators next to a grand staircase. My room was on the tenth deck, so I took the elevator up. Signs inside the elevator advertised the various restaurant options onboard. The doors opened at the tenth deck which resembled an average hotel corridor down which housekeeping were making their way. Since the rooms were still being cleaned, I pressed the button for deck eleven to visit the top deck and enjoy the view of Oslo until it was time.

Passing through the entrance to a conference center, I opened a heavy door to the open air section. Wind flooded in as I stepped out and climbed a short staircase onto the top outside deck. An open air bar at the back of the ship, the Sky Bar, was open for business. I got something to drink and sat next to the edge of the balcony overlooking Akershus Fortress.

Akershus Fortress from the deck of the docked Pearl Seaways

Memories of my walk through the castle grounds came back to me from my vantage point. On the other side of the ship was the Opera House and the Munch Museum. I remembered climbing the Operahuset roof, then walking to the Munch and seeing the Satyricon exhibition. These memories of Oslo would stay with me.

As I sat at my perch, an older man stepped up to the railing and took pictures of the city with a large film camera. He then turned to me.

"Where are you from?" he asked with typical Scandinavian directness.

"Chicago," I said.

I told him about my trip and where I was headed. He was originally from Sweden, but had moved to Copenhagen. The fact that the city was so accessible by bicycle was his main point of praise. Before retirement, he'd been a photographer for boats, so I told him about my trip into the Sognefjord via express boat.

"This is a nice ship," he said, having been on it many times before. "You'll enjoy it."

"It seems like it," I said.

Indeed, I'd have lots to do on my voyage, and I was already impressed with the facilities.

"It's also cool," I said as a manic look took my eyes, a toothy grin forming across my face, "that we're taking the same route as the Vikings — sailing from Norway to Denmark, down the Kattegat!"

By the end of that sentence, my voice had dropped involuntarily into a throaty snarl.

"Enjoy your trip!" the old Swedish man recoiled in terror and moved further down the deck.

Maybe I should've saved that for the book, I thought in bemusement as I finished my drink.

HOW TO HAVE AN ADVENTURE IN SCANDINAVIA

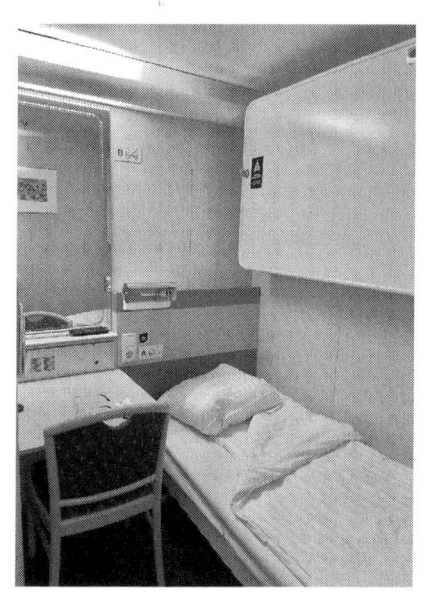

Left:
The author's cabin
on the Pearl Seaways

Enough time had passed for housekeeping to finish, so I took the grand staircase down two floors. My room was mercifully just around the corner from the staircase and elevators at the start of a long hallway. I found it akin to a single business hotel room. I'd stayed in ones of lower quality.

The first thing that came to mind was Amundsen's cabin I'd seen at the Fram Museum just across the way from the where this ship was docked. If a cabin of this sort was good enough for Amundsen for years on end, it was enough for me for a night.

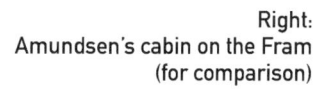

Right:
Amundsen's cabin on the Fram
(for comparison)

RAFFAEL CORONELLI

Bjørvika skyline from the deck of the Pearl Seaways

Bag deposited, I returned topside. It was almost time for the ship to leave. More people had gathered in the bar area, enjoying the sunshine on this sunny day in Oslo.

I stood at the railing on a platform over the bar area. The triangular dry docks of the Fram Museum on Bygdøy were ready to see us off from across the water. The skyline on Bjørvika — Akershus' walls, Operahuset's slopes, and the warped form of the Munch — stood tall in the panorama.

Then, the ship rumbled.

The massive engine whirred to life.

The dock pulled away.

The breeze turned to a stronger gust.

We were heading out onto the Oslofjord, the open mouth of Norway, a gateway to a land where I'd had an unforgettable adventure through unconquerable landscapes and legends.

The Oslofjord churned, calling us out with the tides.

HOW TO HAVE AN ADVENTURE IN SCANDINAVIA

View over the stern of the Pearl Seaways leaving Oslo

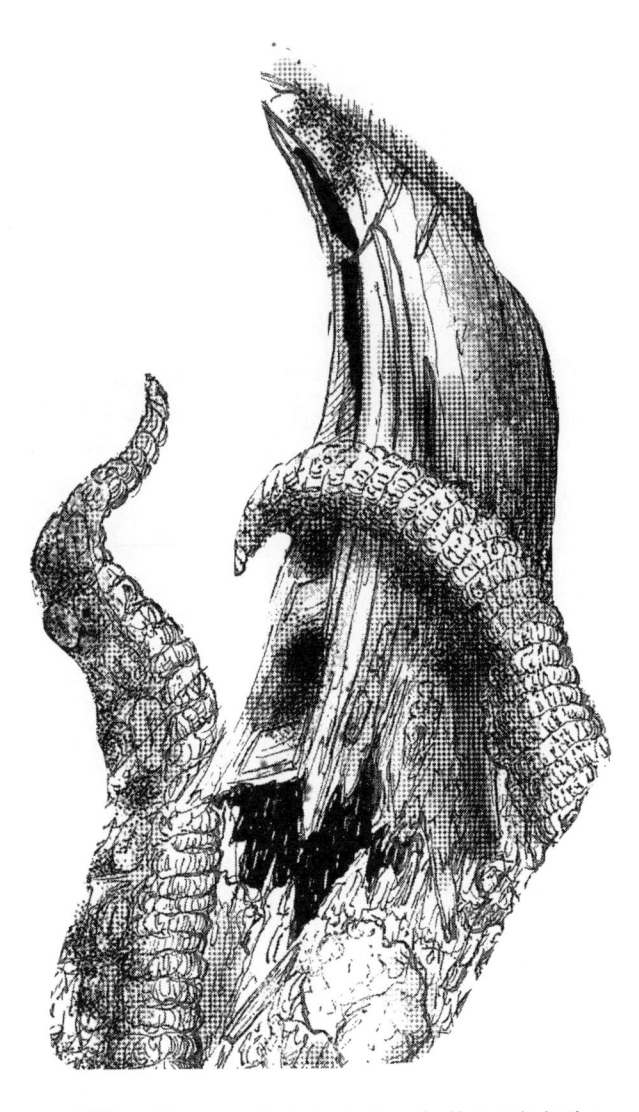

A Viking ship grasped by tentacles from the Kattegat's depths
Illustration by Alex Gayhart

THE KATTEGAT

DFDS Pearl Seaways on the Oslofjord

The Kattegat:
Voyage of Vikings

Mountainous crags moved along either side of the water. The Oslofjord churned forward to the sea. A path sailed by longships in times long past now bore witness to a metal giant carving through the waves.

Built in 1989 at a shipyard in Turku, Finland, the DFDS *Pearl Seaways* had been a mainstay on the high seas for over three decades by the time of my voyage. Refitted as recently as 2018, this 579-foot-long, 2,200-passenger vessel had all the comforts of a modern cruise ship while operating only on a ferry route between Norway and Denmark. As of the most recent refit, it functioned with a state-of-the-art "shorepower" system deriving part of its energy consumption from land-based recharging stations while docked, reducing its carbon footprint.

Its initial route would take it out of the Oslofjord and down the Kattegat, the straight between Norway and Denmark, stopping first at Frederikshavn at the tip of Jutland. From there, it would continue to its destination and the next stop on my trip at Copenhagen. The overnight voyage would take roughly 17 hours.

The first section that would take us out of the 100-kilometer Oslofjord would take several hours in itself. With this much time to kill, I explored the ship's interior.

RAFFAEL CORONELLI

Atrium on decks 7 and 8 of the Pearl Seaways

Most of the ship's decks were dedicated to passenger cabins. Mine was one of the smaller ones, and it was more than enough for me. With a higher ticket price, one could get a room with an outside hull window, a larger bed, or for the especially opulent, a massive suite that would put any of my hotel rooms on the trip to shame.

The entertainment decks, where the most relevant places I'd be spending my time were located, were decks 7 and 8. Exiting the elevator on deck 7, a two-story atrium greeted me. A railing-lined hole in the 8th deck platform allowed for the high ceiling, massive windows displaying a panoramic view of the passing Oslofjord as a background to the proceedings.

To the left, at the bow of the ship, was the 7 Seas restaurant. A reservation is encouraged, so I went and made one at the desk for 7:00 PM. Dinner reservation taken care of, I went in the other direction.

HOW TO HAVE AN ADVENTURE IN SCANDINAVIA

Midship on the starboard side was a coffee bar with seating at porthole windows alongside the lifeboats. Past that, taking up the entirety of the stern section of deck 7, was the duty free shop. Everything from clothing, to toys, to liquor, to bottled water and soft drinks was available at lower prices than on the mainland.

As if to the rescue after my failure to procure a bottle of Norwegian aquavit to bring home, the duty free ship at the stern of the *Pearl Seaways* had a nice selection of mainstream aquavits to choose from, and without the Norwegian alcohol tax. Thus, I got a bottle of Linie for cheaper than I would've on dry land. I'd like to think the crew of the *Fram* would've approved.

Most of the people on the ship were Danish, in line with DFDS being a Danish company and the ship's home port listed on its side as København (the traditional Danish spelling of Copenhagen, in line with with the mumbled pronunciation of everything in the Danish language). The crew all spoke Danish first, and prices were listed in Danish kroner.

Danish pronunciation is harder for me to make out than Norwegian. A number of words in either language are essentially the same thing with different pronunciations, but the Norwegian versions make more phonetic sense to me as a native English-speaker, while Danish has more of a Germanic and consonant-heavy tint. For example, "excuse me" in Norwegian is "*unnskylde*," pronounced like "oonshilda." In Danish, the same word is "*undskyld*," pronounced like "'ndshkll'd."

After returning to my room to deposit the bottle of Linie in my suitcase, I went back down to deck 8.

A model of an older ship operated by DFDS in the era of the *Titanic* sat in a case next to an atrium window, outside which the Oslofjord rolled by. As a port-to-port "cruise ferry," the *Pearl Seaways* is closer in function to the ill-fated White Star Line ship than it is to a cruise ship.

RAFFAEL CORONELLI

At the bow of deck 8 was a higher-end restaurant for the type of passenger staying in the more opulent quarters of the ship. I was fine with the lower restaurant, as it promised an authentic Scandinavian meal. Midship were more eating options, including Little Italy restaurant, the Explorer steakhouse, and two bars — a wine bar, and the more straightforward Navigators bar with seating next to starboard windows like the deck 7 coffee shop. At the stern of deck 8 was a nightclub with live music. Of these places, the Navigators bar piqued my interest the most with its calm seaside views and liquor selection.

Having explored the ship and scoped out places to go later, I headed back topside. The power of Njörðr, Norse god of the wind and the sea, was already proving a challenge for what had been a pleasant day on deck in Oslo harbor. One could feel the fury of the Oslofjord with every gust that blasted across the deck. There were times I had to hold fast to a railing. The wind was so strong that most retreated inside, the outdoor bar shuttering as chairs blew over. The view was unbeatable, though.

The Oslofjord off the stern of the Pearl Seaways

HOW TO HAVE AN ADVENTURE IN SCANDINAVIA

Oscarsborg Fortress

A small fjordside island passed on the starboard. On it was a walled stone structure with cannon positions facing out to sea. It was Oscarsborg Fortress, built in the 19th century, and still active through the Second World War.

On the 9th of April, 1940, the Nazis sent the naval cruiser *Blücher* up the Oslofjord in an attempt to land at the city in coordination with the coup of the Norwegian government. If it landed, it would've allowed the Nazis to take the previous government and King Haakon VII as their prisoners. First, it had to pass Drøbak Sound.

The old cannon mount castle walls of Oscarsborg Festning had been obsolete since the late 19th Century, aside from one key feature — a 20th Century torpedo battery installed by the Norwegian Navy just for an event such as this one. The *Blücher* engaged the fortress, but was unprepared for the water-based torpedos that had been kept secret from German intelligence.

The bombardment from shore began. Holes blasted through the hull of the German cruiser, sending it to the bottom of the fjord. With this small victory, the unseated Norwegian government had the chance they needed to escape to Britain before the arrival of the Nazis in force.

In centuries prior, Drøbak Sound had been the point at which the inner and outer Oslofjord met. This distinction was marked by the way the waters of the fjord would freeze up to Drøbak during the coldest winter months, making passage by smaller ships impossible. In a scenario such as this, longships like those used by the Vikings would leave Drøbak on the journey to Denmark.

With a few hours to kill before dinner, I got out of the wind and descended the grand staircase to deck 8 to have a drink at the Navigators Bar. Like every other facility on the trip, the bar was free of Norwegian or Danish alcohol taxes, making the drinks substantially cheaper than on land — both a welcome and dangerous proposition. I'd have to make sure not to overdo it.

My first choice was a Danish craft beer, Skands Esrum Kloster. This lager-adjacent beer is actually a "klosteryg" beer, a style invented in Northern European monasteries by beer-brewing monks. Its dark color and rich flavor made it look and feel like a dunkel and taste like a variety of herb-enhanced flavors. The fact that it was the cheapest beer I had on the trip is rather absurd, considering the quality, though I understand the reasons.

I sat at a table next to one of the starboard windows watching the outer Oslofjord float by. It was a nice experience, getting the most out of the vessel on which I was bound for the country from which this beer had come.

The traditional combination, at least from what I gathered from my time in Norway, is to have a glass of aquavit and then a beer to follow it up. I was at sea, so I figured I could break the rules on this occasion. Thus, I reversed the combo and my next drink was Linie. I had to have the *Fram* experience of drinking Linie on a ship sailing from Norway, though much further south. As it had been the last time, it was smooth and flavorful, its caramel color brought on by aging on the seas over which I now traveled.

HOW TO HAVE AN ADVENTURE IN SCANDINAVIA

A traditionally shaped glass of Linie aquavit
as the Pearl Seaways exits the Oslofjord

Outside, I watched the Oslofjord reach its end. The boat's movement grew slightly choppier — not enough to knock anything over, as the *Pearl Seaways* was built sturdily enough to avoid that, but noticeably more than it had been inland. We were now no longer in the fjord waters. Ocean stretched as far as the eye could see. The ship had entered the Kattegat.

Norway, Denmark, and Sweden, though not yet defined nations, were all realms of Norse kingdoms during the Viking Age. Travel between them on their longships was facilitated by the Kattegat — the straight between the Skagerrak, which connects to the North Sea from Norway and Jutland's west side, and the Baltic to the East. From the mouth of the Oslofjord all the way down to Denmark's island of Zealand, the Kattegat was the ocean passage that longships would travel from one Viking kingdom to the other. Trade, diplomacy, and the occasional war was conducted via this strip of ocean across which the longships navigated. My most substantial encounter with the Vikings' legacy was ahead in Denmark.

I finished my aquavit just in time for 7:00 PM, the time of my dinner reservation. Descending to the deck below, I entered the 7 Seas restaurant and was promptly seated by an older Danish waiter.

First up was my drink order. I'd just had a Linie, so I figured it was time to enter the realm of the originators of the first style of aquavit. I ordered an Aalborg, the most famous of all Danish aquavits. The specific style was Aalborg Taffel. Upon trying it, it was a bit harsher than what I was used to from the far smoother, aged Norwegian style, but its sharper taste had its own merits and was a good introduction to the Danish wing of the trip.

The 7 Seas was a Scandinavian buffet restaurant. A buffet may not sound glamorous, but this was Scandinavia, and the buffet on *Pearl Seaways* was a full smörgåsbord.

HOW TO HAVE AN ADVENTURE IN SCANDINAVIA

Smörgåsbord are originally from Sweden, but I figured I might as well have one on the high seas between Norway and Denmark with Sweden currently somewhere to the east. All manner of seafood was available, including herring, salmon, muscles, and cod. It was all fresh, all delicious, and perfect for an inter-Scandinavian voyage.

Heartily satisfied with the Smörgåsbord, I paid the waiter and retreated to my cabin. One last look out the atrium windows showed the sky darkening over the Kattegat.

I had hotel rooms on the trip that were less accommodating than my lower-tier ship cabin. It was comfortable, had as much room as I needed, wasn't noisy, and I got a great night's sleep.

In my bunk, the feeling of the ship rocking back and forth was extremely soothing. I wish I could get my bed at home to do that.

It was a far more peaceful experience than what the Vikings would've had on an open longship — especially if they ran into trouble. Ships wrecked and lost on the choppy Nordic seas gave rise to many legends over the years regarding what may lurk in the deep darkness beneath.

The old Norse had tales of a plethora of sea monsters. A whale-like monster said to live near Iceland, the Hafgufa, would lure prey into its gaping maw that appeared on the water like a rim of rocks. Draug were ghosts that sat on the water and capsized passing ships, drowning the crew to join their ranks and become Draug themselves.

One Nordic sea monster in particular has had a lasting impact. Somewhere beneath the dark waves of the Kattegat, tentacles stirred. A beast wholly removed from the vertebrate taxon moved toward the surface, ready to ensnare yet another surface-dwelling target as it had for untold centuries. The Kraken was rising.

RAFFAEL CORONELLI

Illustration by Alex Gayhart

Giant squids are real animals. They are not, however, sinkers of ships or devourers of humans. Architeuthis, the real life inspiration for the Kraken, eat fish and crustaceans and are preyed upon by sperm whales in the dark of the ocean abyss.

It's not impossible that seafarers encountered an Architeuthis on their voyages, or washed up on Norway's shore. Like dinosaur skeletons inspired dragons of European myth, the real giant squid of the deep would've ignited the medieval imagination to create something more sensational, more monstrous than is possible in reality.

The resultant creature was the Kraken. Whispers of a massive sea monster with tentacles capable of crushing vessels and pulling sailors down to be digested passed through the Middle Ages until the 16th Century, when records of seafarers' reported sightings began to be recorded. *"Krake"* in Norwegian roughly means "a gnarled tree," a reference to its long, twisting arms.

HOW TO HAVE AN ADVENTURE IN SCANDINAVIA

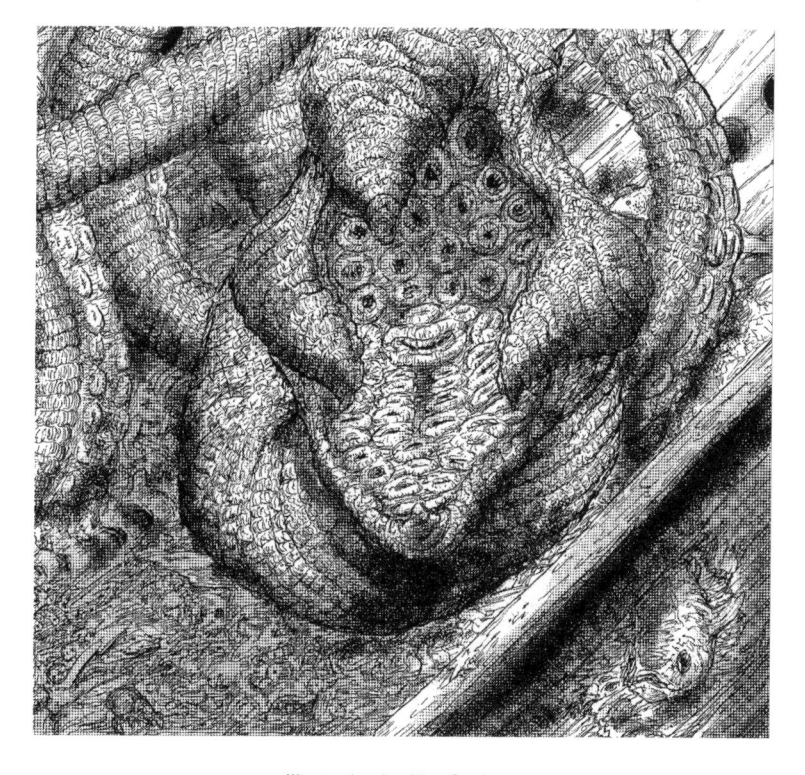

Illustration by Alex Gayhart

Kraken have appeared throughout popular culture since, either as synonymous with a giant squid, or turned into a more sensational sea monster like the Kraken crafted by Ray Harryhausen for the 1981 film *Clash of the Titans*, which substituted the Nordic monster for a previously unnamed beast slain by Greek mythological hero Perseus.

However it is portrayed, the Kraken is a sprawling and ferocious entity. It's the last thing a sailor would want to encounter on the high seas lest they be dragged down into the crushing abyss for a light human snack.

RAFFAEL CORONELLI

The Kraken, drawn by Alex Gayhart

HOW TO HAVE AN ADVENTURE IN SCANDINAVIA

It's easy to imagine great tentacles emerging from the depths of the Kattegat and wrapping around the unsuspecting *Pearl Seaways,* crushing its midship section where I slept into watery oblivion. The starboard atrium windows would shatter, a massive and ferocious invertebrate face outside snapping its beak at the prospect of late-night bar patrons satisfying its hunger. Then it would drag the entire ship below as it had for countless others back to the longships of the Vikings.

The human ships keep getting bigger, the Kraken would think, *but so does my appetite.*

A speaker on my cabin's wall rang out an alarm. A voice announced, first in Danish and then in English, that the *Pearl Seaways* was about to make its first stop at Frederikshavn. It was the middle of the night, and we'd reached Jutland with several more hours to go until our arrival in Copenhagen around 9:00 AM.

I rolled over and went back to sleep while the ship prepared for its stop at Frederikshavn. In spite of any sea monsters, we'd entered the waters of Denmark.

DENMARK

Copenhagen:
Salty Old Queen of the Sea

Sunlight streamed through the windows over the Pearl Seaways' bow from the direction of a city noted as one of the world's happiest places as I strolled into the 7 Seas smörgåsbord restaurant as soon as it opened for breakfast. Showered and hungry, I was ready to get my first day in Denmark started. The buffet was a typical Scandinavian morning feast, with some country-specific additions.

Leverpostej, or pork liver pate, is a culinary staple in Denmark. There's more pork on the menu in Denmark than in Norway because of its proximity to and influence from German cuisine. Jutland has more typical European farms than the upper Scandinavian peninsula, with a climate closer to Central Europe.

Also available was a selection of what might be called "danishes." The term "danish" in the non-Danish world refers to a broad category of items developed at patisseries in Denmark. They usually have a flaky, puffy texture and sweet fillings like custard cream or jam.

The most famous of these pastries, the one Americans would instantly identify as a "danish" is the Spandauer — a circular puff pastry with an open center containing a filling. "Cheese danish," as it's called in the US, is a Spandauer with a cream cheese filling. I'd make sure to call them by their proper names when ordering one; if you ask for a danish in Denmark, you might get a whole person instead.

RAFFAEL CORONELLI

Right:
Danish breakfast
on the Pearl Seaways

In this case, the pastries were out on the buffet with no need to order, so I grabbed a custard creme Spandauer and a slice of Kanelstænger (a long, coffee cake-like pastry with cinnamon and, in this case, a cream custard topping) to have with my pate, herring, and sausages.

My seat by the window gave a panoramic view off the ship's bow overlooking the Kattegat. We were still on our way south past Jutland's eastern seaboard toward the island of Zealand, where resides Copenhagen. In the distance, something was coming up on the starboard side, a piece of land much closer than the far Jutland shore.

HOW TO HAVE AN ADVENTURE IN SCANDINAVIA

Helsingør from the Kattegat with Kronborg Castle on the right

Post-breakfast, I surfaced onto the outside deck and went to the starboard railing. Wind blasted through my hair, threatening to blow my glasses off of my face. Ocean mist sprayed a morning welcome from below.

At the tip of a corner of land sticking out into the Kattegat sat a castle. Ornate towers arose from its by high walls.

Kronborg Castle in the town of Helsingør stood watch at the edge of Zealand. Its cannon positions would've kept an eye on Sweden across the way in centuries past, its walls overlooking the waterway leading to Copenhagen. I'd get a much closer look at Kronborg a couple of days later.

Kronborg Castle welcomed me to the island, and to the next wing of my trip. The castle passed behind us, and I returned below deck momentarily to get a soft drink at the duty free store.

I always want to try local soft drinks from different countries, so I went for one of Denmark's signature ones — a can of Fake Kondi. Sitting on the starboard side of the deck watching the Zealand shore roll by, I cracked open the Fake Kondi and tried the drink. It tasted like 7up; nothing too remarkable. Still, the can was fun, and it was good to try a Danish classic.

Before long, something appeared on the horizon off the bow — a shoreline dotted with buildings. Standing at the railing closest to the front of the ship to get a better look, I watched it grow closer.

RAFFAEL CORONELLI

Copenhagen from the harbor

The *Pearl Seaways* sailed through the harbor and up to the quay. Strains of Danny Kay singing "Wonderful Copenhagen" played in my head. A domed building, Marmorkirken, was the first landmark I could make out. Canals stretched inland, lined by colorful buildings. Pleasure boats roamed the waterfront. Already, this city's good vibes emanated from the shore.

With the ship about to dock, I headed down to my room to collect my things. A crowd gathered on deck 5 to disembark at the port. The ship docked, the crew secured the exit ramp, and after a few short minutes, I was crossing the bridge onto Zealand — my home for three days.

Taxis waited by the DFDS terminal for passengers, but I decided I'd walk the five kilometers to the hotel. It was a long way just to put my luggage down, but I wanted to see as much as possible on my entrance to the city. This would prove to be a walking tour in itself, a journey from the port down the main waterway through iconic sights.

This main waterway is the space between the two islands that constitute the city of Copenhagen. The main part of the city is on the east shore of Zealand. Across the way are the city's neighborhoods on the comparatively tiny southeastern island of Amager. Beyond Amager is another waterway, across which lies the Swedish city of Malmö.

HOW TO HAVE AN ADVENTURE IN SCANDINAVIA

Copenhagen's metropolitan area unofficially constitutes much of the greater Øresund region that bridges the cross-Øresund straight border between the two countries. Malmö is as close as a suburb to Copenhagen despite itself being the third largest city in Sweden. Altogether, the area has a population of around four million people, which is rather disproportionately large compared with other population centers in Scandinavia.

Most apparent in contrast with Norway was the bright sunshine that shone the colorful city in all its highlights.

The first stop on my self-guided walking tour was Langelinie, a shoreline park. Copenhagen is home to copious amounts of walkable parkland.

Just inside the park stood the Maritime Monument, a bronze statue of a winged goddess standing atop a base carved with reliefs. The monument was built in memory of Danish sailors lost during the First World War.

The Maritime Monument

RAFFAEL CORONELLI

A row of bicycles zoomed past me on the path. These walkable areas make the city massively popular with legions of roving cyclists, which can keep you on your toes as a pedestrian trying to avoid getting mowed down. Bicycles are vehicles, after all, so be careful.

Ahead, a large crowd gathered around a spot on the waterfront. Moving closer, I peered through them to get a look. It was the statue of the Little Mermaid, a symbol of the city based on Danish author Hans Christian Andersen's famous 1837 story, one of the country's most famous contributions to world culture.

"The Little Mermaid," like many of Andersen's stories, has remained embedded in the public consciousness thanks to near two centuries of publishing, retelling, and adaptation in forms as far reaching as Japanese magical girl anime series. For the city, the statue is a guardian at the edge of the sea, a symbol of the amphibious nature of Copenhagen as it connects to the canals that filter the waters of the Kattegat through the city's heart.

Left:
The Little Mermaid statue

HOW TO HAVE AN ADVENTURE IN SCANDINAVIA

Gefion Fountain

On the southern side of the park was the Gefion Fountain. This impressive turn-of-the-20th-century fountain is topped by a sculpture of the Norse agriculture goddess Gefjon driving a plough pulled by oxen. Out of the Nordic countries, Gefjon seems to have given most of her attention to Denmark; its hospitable climate makes it a far more productive place to grow things than further north.

RAFFAEL CORONELLI

*Right:
Statues of
Hermès and Poseidon at the
Royal Pavillon*

At the southern edge of Langelinie Park was the Royal Pavilion, home to Greek-inspired marble sculptures. Among them was a gate featuring the Greek gods Hermès and Poseidon on either side. Passing through the gate, I headed inland for a bit to see one of the main sights I'd spotted from the ship on the way in.

A row of rococo buildings lined each side of a street leading to an archway supported by columns. Through the columns stood uniformed guards. Perfectly still and wearing large, fluffy black bearskin hats, they were the spitting image of the royal guards in London. The comparison wasn't far off, as their purpose was similar — they were the royal guards of Denmark, and the expansive courtyard onto which I'd entered was the Amalienborg, a ring of palaces home to the Danish royal family.

HOW TO HAVE AN ADVENTURE IN SCANDINAVIA

Equestrian statue of Frederik V at Amalienborg

At one end of the courtyard was Marmorkirken, the Marble Church, completed nearly a hundred years after the palaces in the 17th Century. This was the dome I'd seen from the ship. The four palaces around Amalienborg date to the 16th Century and are still in use by the royals, hence the guards on duty. At the courtyard's center was a bronze equestrian statue of Frederik V overlooking his descendants' home from podium-mounted horseback.

Left:
Marmorkirken

265

RAFFAEL CORONELLI

Nyhavn

Less than a kilometer down Toldbodgade was a bridge over one of Copenhagen's most famous canals — Nyhavn. Midway out onto Nyhavnbroen bridge, I had to stop and take in the view. Brightly colored buildings lined the waterway, pleasure boats and floating bars dotting the canal. It was an image that one would show to convince you that Copenhagen was a land of pure fun.

For such a bright, happy place, it actually has a rather dark origin. King Christian V of Denmark made captured Swedish war prisoners dig the canal as forced labor in the 1670s. Despite this, it became a pleasure center for most of its history, as it clearly remains today. Hans Christian Andersen even lived on the canal in his 40s and 50s.

After Nyhavnbroen was Christian IV's bridge, named after the predecessor to the Swede-enslaving canal builder. The bridge leads to Slotsholmen, "castle islet." This small island is cut off from the shore by a pair of canals and is named as such because it houses Christiansborg Slot.

HOW TO HAVE AN ADVENTURE IN SCANDINAVIA

Børsen (left) and Christiansborg Slot (right)

 Christiansborg is a baroque 20th Century palace and the seat of Danish government. Built in the style of older Danish palaces, Christiansborg is a more modern construction than castles I'd see elsewhere on Zealand.
 A green corkscrew tower stuck out of the top of a low-lying neighboring building. A much older building from the 17th Century, this was Børsen, or Christian IV's stock exchange. Børsen still serves as the location of the Danish Chamber of Commerce. The twin pointed towers of Børsen and Christiansborg gave Castle Islet an iconic image to go along with its status as the still-in-use seat of Danish power.

Frederiksholms Kanal

Further southwest lay the Vesterboro neighborhood, where I'd be staying. The first order of business was to drop off my luggage at the hotel. The hotel wasn't much to write about, the cheapest budget hotel of the trip.

This was a cut cost on my part. These decisions can keep travel affordable, but I can't say I'd recommend this particular place. They didn't clean the room between nights and it was overbooked and noisy. The lobby was so packed it felt like an airport terminal for lost hotel patrons who'd all decided to stay at the cheapest place possible.

Luggage deposited, I headed out to explore the neighborhood. Bernstorffsgade, a main boulevard, lead inland. Joyous screams and laughter drifted out of an area on the northeast side marked by a gate shaped like a mountain. This was one of Copenhagen's major landmarks, Tivoli Gardens; an old fashioned amusement park and pleasure garden from the 19th Century that's remained largely the same as it was on opening. I'd planned to spend my evening there, easy to get to from the hotel.

Across the street from Tivoli was Copenhagen Central Station. A sprawling, ornate, turn of the 20th Century building, the station is more architecturally memorable than Oslo's. It fits well with the city's aesthetic and its positioning across from Tivoli, which had been open at the location for more than half a century by the time the station was built.

In the area in front of the train station, I spotted a Copenhagen staple. I hadn't eaten since my ship breakfast, so I figured I could go for a midday snack, and this was the place to do it.

Denmark is the land of lunch. When your national delicacy is the open-faced sandwich, the populace seems to get caught in the midday meal's gravitational pull. Luckily, this means that there are tons of affordable lunch options to choose from that'll get you through the day.

HOW TO HAVE AN ADVENTURE IN SCANDINAVIA

John's Hotdog Deli

In front of the Central Station, I happened upon a pølsevogn (Danish-style hot dog stand) that I'd actually seen recommended before — John's Hotdog Deli. This name doesn't sound like it would be the most authentic Copenhagen eatery, but nothing is more authentic than being served a Danish-style street sausage by John Hotdogs himself. That probably was not the name of the guy in the stand (which is named after its founder John Michael Jensen) but let's pretend it is.

John's Hotdog Deli had several menu options, including the "Fransk" dog, or French style, with a sausage sticking out of a hole in a long, hollow bun. I have never heard of French people actually eating sausages like this, but that's what the Danish call it. There were German style sausages, which makes sense due to close geographic proximity. The main attraction, though, was the "rød" — a Danish pork sausage with bright red skin on a bun with various trappings. This is a Copenhagen classic, and was the one I had to try.

RAFFAEL CORONELLI

Giving my order for a rød with everything on it, I watched John Hotdogs assemble the delicacy, taking the rød sausage out of a boiling vat and plastering it with goodies. I stood and ate it in the vicinity, pigeons gathering nearby and hoping for me to be a sloppy eater. Unfortunately for them, I enjoyed every bite of the rød. It was an unmissable taste of Copenhagen, the work of a true artisan at his craft.

When coming to and from the train station later in the trip, I'd return to this spot where John Hotdogs' magic cart normally resides, only to find it vanished into the aether. Perhaps it only appears to us at certain times, momentarily visible to the mortal realm. Whatever the case, I'd enjoyed one of Copenhagen's lunch classics.

Right:
Rød Pølse
from John's Hotdog Deli

HOW TO HAVE AN ADVENTURE IN SCANDINAVIA

Left:
Rodin's "The Thinker"
in the Carlsberg Glyptotek
garden

Off the southeast side of Tivoli is a large museum building — the Carlsberg (like the beer) Glyptotek. I didn't have time to go inside this famous Copenhagen art museum, but the museum made up for it with an outdoor sculpture garden.

The centerpiece of this free-to-wander space was Rodin's "The Thinker," perched in thought on a pedestal in front of the south facade. The Thinker had picked the perfect spot to do his thinking; this peaceful garden was a respite from the bustling city, filled in the warmer months like the one in which I visited with colorful flowers to accompany the art pieces. There's even a lovely sculpture of a demonic "Troll that smells Christian blood."

Right:
"Troll that Smells Christian Blood"
by Niels Hansen Jacobsen
in the Carlsberg Glyptotek garden

RAFFAEL CORONELLI

Right:
The Rådhus clock tower

My last, brief self-guided tour stop in the was the Rådhuspladsen, or City Hall Square, off the park's northeast side. The Rådhus was another turn-of-the-20th-Century brick building with an ornate design and a clock tower. The plaza in front was a sunny, open area.

Crossing the plaza in front of the City Hall, I saw at least two sausage stands. I hadn't heard of these, and while I'm sure they're perfectly fine, I'm glad my first experience with a Copenhagen street sausage was from the legendary Hotdogs John, hero of Denmark.

Whereas Oslo was a near-hellish experience to navigate but had a bunch of unmissable things in it, Copenhagen was the opposite. As I was quickly discovering, the best way to get the most out of the city was to go walk around and enjoy the good vibes.

My wandering northwest from Tivoli, to which I'd return that evening, took me into the Meat Packing District. This name might not sound terribly appealing, but it refers to the former use of the 1900s-era warehouses that constitute its architecture. Today, this area is home to microbreweries, bars, and all things related to Copenhagen's beer culture.

HOW TO HAVE AN ADVENTURE IN SCANDINAVIA

Copenhagen is the home of Carlsberg, the light and mild Pilsner enjoyed the world over. The Carlsberg empire was a source of funding for much of the city's current pedestrian-friendly planning, as its owners made sure their garden city was up to their own standards. Carlsberg is fine, but you'll find more delicious craft beer in the Meat Packing District, as I was about to discover.

Weaving through the back alleys and past the occasional bar's outdoor seating area, I wove further into the district's brick maze. Sounds of revelers echoed off the cobblestones. Then, around a corner, a banner hung announcing a discovery — "Mikkeler Beer Celebration."

What luck! By wandering aimlessly, I'd found a beer festival with free admission!

Grabbing a delicious porter from one of the tents, I stood and enjoyed it on the sunny cobblestones outside the Mikkeler brewery. Copenhagen's warm vibes had proven it a great place to clink and drink one down. As I found upon later research, the beer festival is held each year in May. Plan accordingly if you'd like to attend. I was glad to have found it at random.

Finished with my beer, I returned briefly to my hotel to check in, change my clothes, and then get ready for the evening. I was ready for the Tivoli experience.

Right:
Mikkeler Beer Celebration

RAFFAEL CORONELLI

Entrance to Tivoli

The ticket office sat under the mountain at Tivoli's entrance on the train station side. An older man inside sold me an admission ticket, which was only $16. Rides cost extra and have individual tickets, but I was there for the "pleasure garden" aspect, not the amusement park.

A pleasure garden is an old fashioned concept that used to be common in 19th Century Europe. It's essentially a nicely decorated place for adults to eat, drink, walk around freely. This is Tivoli's main purpose in the evening, though you can of course still go on the rides if you choose.

An artificial waterfall greeted me on the other side of the artificial mountain as I crossed the park's threshold. It was crowded, but not packed, and already I noticed more places to eat and drink than what one would expect at an amusement park.

I attended in the midst of the 2022 Tivoli Food Festival. In addition to a summer-long series of events with celebrity chef guests taking a stage, the park was highlighting gourmet food in their more than thirty restaurants, sixteen-option food hall, and seventeen coffee and sweets shops. This was good news for me as I searched out a place to have dinner while enjoying the park's vibes.

HOW TO HAVE AN ADVENTURE IN SCANDINAVIA

"Tivoli Nights! Oh, what a sight!"
So sings a musical number about the park in 1961 Danish cinema classic *Reptilicus*, a film about a gigantic dragon resembling one from northern European legends that takes on the Danish military, lays waste to Copenhagen, vomits acid, eats people, and advertises Danish tourism. This unusually placed song in the early part of the film tells of Tivoli's vibrant nightlife as a pleasure garden, at least until Reptilicus later destroys it.

Past the center of the park, a certain area caught my eye. A tall, red pagoda inspired by Japanese architecture stood next to a torii gate. This foreign architecture was part of Tivoli's original appeal — by making it look like far away places, the 19th Century Danish could travel while in the heart of Copenhagen. Now it feels rather quaint, but there's something charming about it.

Left:
Tivoli Gardens

RAFFAEL CORONELLI

Daemonen coaster at Tivoli

Inside this area was a street decorated in the same vaguely Asian architectural style. A Chinese-style dragon hung over it on the side of a roller coaster.
Reptilicus lives! I thought to myself.

It was in this area that I stopped to buy a beer at one of the stands. I got a Royal Pilsner (brewed in Denmark) and enjoyed it while walking the grounds. As a pleasure garden, Tivoli is a great place to have a cold, alcoholic drink while taking a walk.

A galleon sat in a quiet lagoon on the other side of the pagoda. More buildings resembling those of far off lands like India dotted the park. Being from the US, traditional Denmark has its own exoticism, but this was all fun to see. I kept on the lookout for a good Danish restaurant.

HOW TO HAVE AN ADVENTURE IN SCANDINAVIA

At last, I found one. All it took to draw me in was a sign advertising a special "aquavit menu." They didn't have to tell me twice!

The restaurant was Grøften, a seafood-focused Scandinavian restaurant. Seated by a window looking out at the park, my friendly waiter agreed to help me me with the special menu by recommending aquavits to try with the different courses. I could already tell this would be one of the trip's better dinners.

The first course featured a smørrebrød with pickled herring on rye bread. The aquavit pairing was a Danish brand, O.P. Anderson Klar Krydret. Its hints of dill went well with the meal's ingredients.

Right:
The Aquavit Menu
(first course)
at Grøften in Tivoli

RAFFAEL CORONELLI

My second aquavit of the meal was recommended specially by the waiter as a personal favorite of his. It was Brøndum Kummenaquavit, also Danish. This one was flavored with cumin, giving it an extremely interesting smoky flavor that went with the second course — smørrebrød with cooked herring shredded together with a mashed potato purée reminiscent of Bergen plukkfisk.

To say nothing of the aquavits, the meal was a wonderful foray into gourmet level open-faced Danish sandwiches. Smørrebrød are not really sandwiches, but that's the closest English approximation, as they have ingredients on a slice of bread. In Danish, the name literally means "butter and bread." This is the most emblematic food of Denmark, and all the ingredients were excellent.

"More food?" the waiter asked on returning.

I felt like I was going to explode after the potato and herring smørrebrød, but I did want another aquavit.

"Does more come with what I ordered?!" I inquired, skeptical.

"You can have as much as you want!" he said.

"Just as long as it's not as big," I conceded.

"They're scaled down," he assured me.

Left:
Aquavit Menu
(second course)
at Grøften

HOW TO HAVE AN ADVENTURE IN SCANDINAVIA

The third aquavit he brought was Aalborg Grill, also distilled from cumin and anise. I enjoyed this one a lot more than the basic Aalborg Taffel I'd had on the ship the previous night.

I have to be honest — that third food course was one too many. I couldn't even finish it, a rare thing for me as something of a fan of food. This was just too much.

The waiter told me that two Americans had complained that he had been rude to them, and asked if I'd gotten that impression. I said not at all, and that I found it bizarre that they would say that. He'd given a perfectly amicable introduction to Danish aquavit and I appreciated his recommendations and his friendly service. There's just no pleasing some people, but it could also have been an artifact of cultural differences — the Danish are direct in their speech to the point of being terse, even more than Norwegians. You have to understand that the tone is not meant to be harsh.

After my wonderful dinner at Grøften, I walked a bit more around the park to get enough of an appetite back before having a tiny cup of stracciatella gelato. It wouldn't be a complete Tivoli experience without something from one of the confection stands.

Altogether, my evening at Tivoli cost me about 70 bucks (USD). I'd call that more than worth it.

Leaving the park, I thought back on the jam-packed day. Copenhagen had greeted me with all of its splendor, good vibes, and excellent food and drink. Its status as one of the happiest places in the world made perfect sense.

Copenhagen, wonderful, wonderful,
Copenhagen for me!

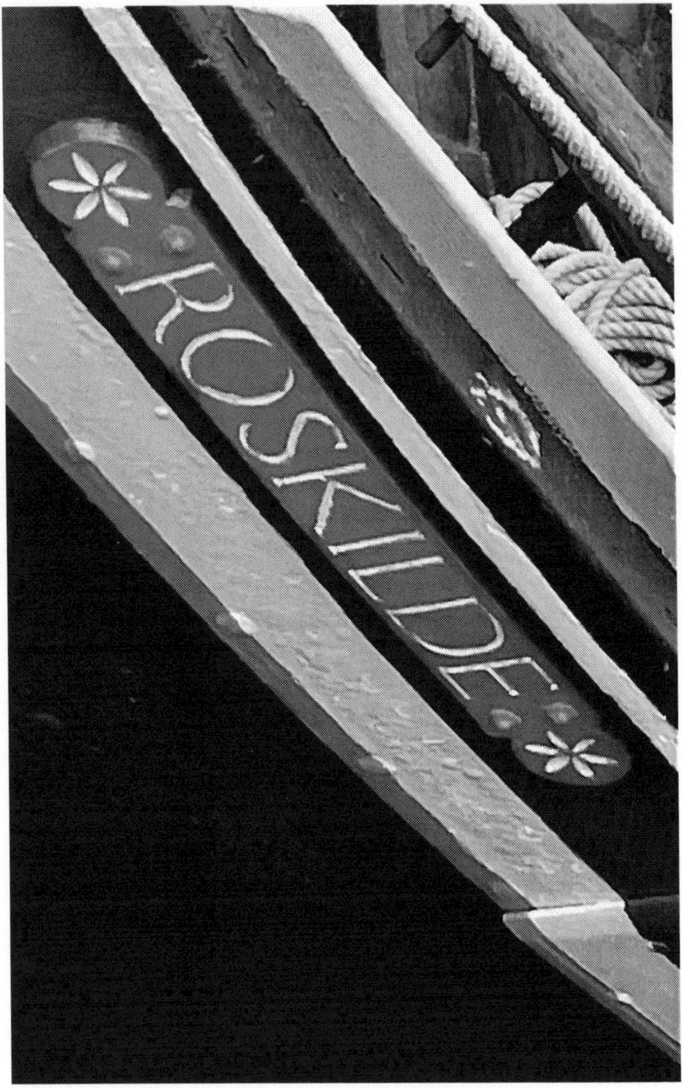
ROSKILDE

Roskilde:
Bay of Longships

Vikings are synonymous with Scandinavian history. In this book, I've talked about Norse mythology and visited important places from the Viking Age. However, it's been relatively light on tangible Viking presence up to this point. That's because my trip's most prominent encounter with their legacy was in Roskilde, Denmark.

Up bright and early, I made the short walk from my hotel to Copenhagen Central Station. I'd be taking the first train available out to the town midway across Zealand. For my within-Denmark travel, I'd gotten a three-day rail pass using the Eurail app. It was an excellent, cost-saving deal, even with a first-class pass that allowed me to sit in the nicest part of the train.

The first train to Roskilde had been slightly rescheduled for whatever reason, so I grabbed a coffee and a pastry in the station for a quick breakfast. Soon enough, I was boarding the first class car.

In addition to a first class on longer distance trains, all Danish trains including Metro have a "quiet car". This is for people to sit and enjoy silence, where talking or making noise is prohibited. These cars feel highly civilized in both concept and execution. Sometimes you just want quiet!

RAFFAEL CORONELLI

First class on the Copenhagen-Roskilde line

From my seat in the otherwise empty first class, I watched the west end of Copenhagen roll by until it had turned to the countryside. Outside the city, Zealand was a pleasant suburbia filled with old world buildings and lush greenery. The train from Copenhagen to Roskilde was the very first railway line in Denmark, starting off the day on an appropriately historical note.

A medieval market town, Roskilde has been a center of commerce for at least a millennium. It sits at the back of Roskilde Fjord, the most defensible port in Denmark. This feature gave it importance in the Viking Age, and facilitated the archeological finds that fueled this chapter.

My introduction to the town was through Denmark's oldest railway station. Roskilde Station dates to the 1840s, the end point of Denmark's aforementioned first rail line.

HOW TO HAVE AN ADVENTURE IN SCANDINAVIA

The original station remains in use. Of course, more tracks have been added over the years to accommodate more than just the original.

Turning right out of the station's main entrance onto Hestetorvet, I continued onto a foot path into the town's idyllic park system. When walking anywhere in Denmark, you'll inevitably end up on well-maintained parkland.

The Roskilde Vikingeskibsmuseet (Viking Ship Museum) is situated at the harbor on the edge of the fjord, the point from which the Danish Vikings would launch into voyages and into battle. Immediately noticeable is that the harbor itself is part of the museum, and is home to a fleet of reconstructed Viking ships. This feature allows for one of the most unique experiences available in Denmark, for which I'd buy a ticket for that afternoon.

First, I had to go inside. As the museum tells, the story of the Viking ships at Roskilde — the Skuldelev ships — is the reason for the place's existence.

In the early 20th Century, word emerged from local fishermen that the remains of a "medieval ship" lay at the bottom of Roskilde fjord. One fisherman retrieved a part of this ship, bringing it to the surface and keeping it in his home. It wasn't quite like other medieval ships that had been found, because it was in fact much older — a relic of a prior age. The Danish government showed some interest, but were preoccupied.

World War II brought hardship to Denmark. With a lack of resources in the hard Danish winter, the fisherman who'd brought up part of the ship was forced to burn it as firewood. Thus, the only example of what exactly lay on the seabed off Roskilde was destroyed.

In the 1960s, interest renewed as divers discovered exactly what these "medieval ships" were. They were Viking longships, the most complete artifacts of such vessels Denmark had ever seen.

RAFFAEL CORONELLI

Denmark was the place of Nordic culture's origin. While its remnants are spread across the Scandinavian peninsula, Denmark was where the first Vikings lived and migrated into the north. This was a meaningful find for the region, country, and those who studied its civilization.

Divers and archaeologists painstakingly retrieved the ships from the bottom of the fjord using cutting edge techniques. From there, they were able to reconstruct the pieces on metal frames like dinosaur skeletons. These are the resurrected ships on display inside the museum.

The ships, made from the original materials that have survived the ravages of time, are still awe-inspiring to see in person. These ships traversed oceans and helped build Scandinavian civilization. Some of them were built as far away as Norway and sailed the route I'd come on my way to Denmark before finding their resting place at the bottom of the bay at the back of Roskilde Fjord.

The museum's rules on licensing photography of the ships are fairly strict, which is why you're not seeing pictures of these magnificent vessels published in this book. These are treasures for those who visit, or to see online in Instagram resolution.

After viewing these magnificent original vessels inside the museum, I headed outside to the harbor where resided the second part of the museum's work. Moored along the piers lining the harbor at the back of the fjord were wooden ships built in the Viking style. Some of these were 1:1 recreations of the ships I'd just seen inside that had been lifted out of the fjord from the Viking Age.

Based on the recovered artifacts, experts at the museum have spent the past half-century studying Viking shipbuilding techniques. Using original construction methods, the museum has funded the construction of new versions of these ancient ships based on evidence gleaned from these discoveries combined with knowledge of traditional shipbuilders from across Scandinavia.

HOW TO HAVE AN ADVENTURE IN SCANDINAVIA

As I stated in a prior chapter, northern Norwegian fishermen kept building fishing boats using the techniques of Viking longships into the 1940s. These techniques are on display in Roskilde harbor, as the museum has brought in experts from northern Norway to work on their reconstructions.

There's even a 20th Century Lofoten fishing boat on display in the harbor with a basic hull shape remarkably close to the Viking vessels. I thought back to my dinner at Lofotstua, and how the fishermen responsible for that were part of a lineage stretching directly back to the Viking longship builders.

What separates Viking shipbuilding from other techniques of the era or after is the layout of the wooden planks and how they're connected to form the hull. In other wooden ships' hulls, the planks are bolted flat, end to end. In a Viking ship, the wooden planks overlap each other to create a sturdier hull that's harder to breach.

The winding, twisting shape of the fjord made it the perfect place to fortify. This was why the Danish Vikings made Roskilde a stronghold and kept a fleet at the rear of the bay. Enemies had no way to make it through the fjord without setting off the alarm, fires ignited by watchmen that would alert everyone to the oncoming enemy. The ships and defenses would be ready before anyone could get close.

As I inspected the ships on the harbor, a man roughly my age approached me and asked if I was a museum guest. I confirmed and showed him my admission bracelet. He informed me that he was a shipbuilder and would be doing a free guided tour of the harbor at 3:00 that afternoon. I of course was interested and told him I'd be there. The harbor was also home to a restaurant that served a modern approximation of what Vikings actually ate, which is of course where I planned to eat later.

First on the agenda for the afternoon was the activity for which I'd bought a ticket, the thing that had drawn me to Roskilde more than anything else — sailing out onto the fjord in a reconstructed Viking longship.

The time on my ticket wasn't for another half hour, so I enjoyed walking around the seaside harbor in the mean time. Aside from the ships, the fjord itself was incredibly scenic. Sun beamed down on the water as gentle waves rolled in with a cool breeze. Roskilde fjord was another idyllic place to spend a day.

Little by little, a small group of guests gathered near the restaurant where the group was to meet. It was an eclectic crew of tourists, locals, and other enthusiasts. Among them were a number of people with English accents, tourists hoping to recreate the ancient voyages that famously stormed their own shores in the Middle Ages.

A young Danish woman led us into a wooden building full of sailing supplies. She instructed us of what the process of boarding would be like and had us put our bags in storage before donning life vests. After, we filed out to one of the reconstructed ships moored at the dock.

Every seat in the boat was filled. Every member of the makeshift crew had their own heavy, steady oar, facing toward the rear of the ship. I was near the stern, where the rowing instructor stood and gave us direction. She explained that we'd have to row in synchronicity on her mark, and that the port side would go first to get us away from the shore. Her instructions were clear, leaving little reason for error.

The port side oars rowed, then the starboard where I sat. The boat creaked and glided through the water. Soon we were off into Roskilde Fjord, just as the Vikings had set off in centuries past.

HOW TO HAVE AN ADVENTURE IN SCANDINAVIA

The author of this book in a Viking ship on Roskilde Fjord

RAFFAEL CORONELLI

Hoisting the sail on Roskilde Fjord

HOW TO HAVE AN ADVENTURE IN SCANDINAVIA

I expected rowing a Viking longship to be difficult. On the contrary, it glided gracefully with each swing of the oars. The hardest part was keeping everyone in the same rhythm, but soon the inexperienced crew got the hang of it with the help of our seasoned instructor.

Blazing sun beamed down on Denmark's best defended fjord. The rhythm of the oars beat the water like drums of war. I was a thousand years back in time. Odin was guiding our ship, our axes, spears, and swords. (We didn't have any of those, but we at least had the ship.)

About midway out onto the bay, the instructor told us to stop rowing and retract our oars. It was time to hoist the sail. It so happened that by virtue of sitting in the right place, the instructor chose me to stand up and pull one of the ropes on her command.

"Wait just two seconds," she told me as I pulled a little too soon.

It had something to do with keeping the starboard side of the sail in place while those toward the front of the ship fastened it. Everyone had to be in place first.

"Okay," she said, "now!"

Standing in the ship and pulling a rope, I watched the square, khaki-colored Viking sail open on the mast. The ocean breeze blew my hair back. I held fast to the rope, legs in a stance that kept me from falling overboard. It all had a certain forearm-flexing, blood-pumping thrill.

Wind filled the sail and carried us across the water. Ocean spray and the cool breeze followed the sail-hoisting with a brief pleasure cruise in this Viking-style boat with no propulsion but what its original designers would've had.

Between the relative smoothness of rowing and the way the wind shot the ship forward, I was surprised at how well the ship handled being on the ocean. It shouldn't have been a surprise at all — these were ships that crossed the Kattegat to Norway, the North Atlantic to Iceland, Greenland, and Newfoundland.

RAFFAEL CORONELLI

Left:
The author of this book on Roskilde Fjord

The wind was blowing in, which nullified the need to row back to shore. Our raid would have to wait for another day. Taking the sail down, we rowed the short distance back into the harbor and moored the boat where we'd found it.

Collecting my bag back afterward, I thanked the instructor for the great trip, telling her it was "awesome." I meant it — it was one of the most memorable experiences I had in Denmark, true-to-life Viking action in modern day.

I'd worked up an appetite with all the rowing and sail-hoisting, so I moseyed in to Cafe Knarr. This cafe operated by the museum serves up a menu of recreated Viking food. Historians and culinary experts have determined the kind of things people in the Viking Age actually ate, which Cafe Knarr has turned into dishes that are edible and appetizing to modern humans. All ingredients are things that were on hand in Viking times, and the dishes are traditional.

I ordered the Viking Plank, an assortment platter that would give me a mid-afternoon feast, as this meal would be functioning as an early dinner. To drink, I ordered mead.

HOW TO HAVE AN ADVENTURE IN SCANDINAVIA

Mead was the drink of the Vikings. I'd never had it before, so I was in for a surprise. When one thinks of what Vikings drank after a long, hard day of raiding, one imagines beer or something harder. Mead is more like cider or mulled wine, and has a sweet taste derived from fermented honey. I liked it, but it was not what I expected.

The food platter consisted of meatballs, cheese, smoked halibut, cured ham, lingonberry compote, a cabbage salad, and rye bread. It was all delicious, but it sparked an amusing thought — this was Norwegian food. Danish historians had done their best to reconstruct what the Vikings ate, and what it ended up being was Norwegian cuisine. Go figure! The meal was excellent and a worthy addition to a day of Viking shenanigans.

Left:
Viking food at Cafe Knarr

RAFFAEL CORONELLI

I had a bit of time until the free guided tour of the boat building yard, so I took a walk past the museum's limit on the waterfront. The rest of the harbor was charming in itself. A seaside path wound around the bay into a forest further down. I walked to the start of the forest path and turned back, not wanting to stray too far.

By 3:00, I was back at the shipbuilders' workshop. The guide I'd met there before was ready to start the tour. He told of how the ships are rebuilt every few years or so, partly because updated information about their construction in Viking times helps inform the way a reconstruction can be better done. The museum also likes to have a boat under construction at all times, just to have something to show off and keep the builders employed.

One of the most interesting anecdotes he revealed was that archeological knowledge of Viking culture comes from second-hand sources, as Viking runes weren't typically used to record information of practical use. Tools for shipbuilding, he explained, are known to have been in use at certain times due to their presence in the Bayeux Tapestry — the sprawling piece of French-English medieval art that depicts the 1066 Norman invasion of Britain.

A Viking ship from the Bayeux Tapestry

HOW TO HAVE AN ADVENTURE IN SCANDINAVIA

The guide was from Norway, and had been brought to the museum due to his shipbuilding expertise. He was the latest generation of Norwegian shipbuilders who'd held onto the Viking techniques, and was putting that knowledge to use for the sake of historical preservation. As a Norwegian, he had a few hilarious jokes about the Danish language, and something about the Danish drinking beer instead of water during the Middle Ages.

It was a greatly informative session, and I appreciated his expertise. Like the other staff at the museum, he was bringing the true experience of the Viking Age to life in a much more comfortable and less violent setting.

At that, I left Roskilde Fjord behind. The place had been a time portal, worth the entire day I'd dedicated to it. The sailing trip, the food, the locale, and the ships themselves were an invaluable way to immerse in the most iconic chapter of Scandinavia's premodern history.

The next day, I'd move forward in time to an age of castles.

Frederiksborg Castle from the Castle Lake

Frederiksborg and Kronborg: Castles of Zealand

Back in the train station first thing the next morning, my first order of business was to buy a sandwich for the road. I figured I'd try something different on my way to the day's first attraction — have a one-man bench picnic in a Hillerød, Denmark park.

The train tore north out of Copenhagen. Green fields and brush rolled by as we entered the upper corner of Zealand. This would be the area of the island in which I'd spend the entire day, as it was home to two of Denmark's most important and magnificent castles.

Within the half hour, I arrived in Hillerød. A charming mid-sized town, Hillerød was a home to monarchs in the 17th and 18th Centuries via the looming presence of Frederiksborg Castle.

Similarly to my arrival in Roskilde, it didn't take long to reach a lush public park. A short way in, the trees opened and an incredible sight revealed itself.

Ducks swam on the surface of a shimmering lake reflecting the morning sun. It was a lovely spot, but that could hardly draw my attention from the other side.

Dominating the scene from across the water was an ornate, green-roofed fortress. A belfry tower stood above its walls, supported midway up by golden metal balls, with four obelisks around it. This structural marvel stood out to me almost as much as it must have to Danish peasants upon the castle's building in the 17th Century. If I were living in 1620 and had to guess where the King lived with no prior information, the building with golden balls holding up its tower would've been my first guess.

RAFFAEL CORONELLI

A recurring theme for my trip, the castle didn't open until 10:00. This gave me enough time to sit on a bench facing the lake and munch down on my sandwich. With only the ducks on the water to accompany me, I enjoyed brunch in perfect view of one of Denmark's most scenic castles.

A significant moat drew water in from the lake. The bridge over it was well fortified. I crossed the bridge and under the gate's archway, taking me into the first magnificent courtyard.

Water sprayed skyward across the vista of the castle's front, bronze statues of Greek gods congregating like a scene on Mount Olympus. The centerpiece of this forecourt, the Neptune Fountain depicted Neptune as a symbol of the King of Denmark, proclaiming him king of the Nordic seas.

Neptune Fountain at Frederiksborg Castle

HOW TO HAVE AN ADVENTURE IN SCANDINAVIA

Left:
Frederiksborg Castle
Belfry from the inner courtyard

Past the Neptune Fountain, a second gated wall arose to ward off intruders. I entered and found myself in the inner courtyard. From this inside vantage point, I was treated to a close-up view of the belfry tower I'd admired from across the lake. Admission covered more than than just the fully furnished castle interior. Frederiksborg is home to the Museum of National History, an extensive collection that makes use of the castle's rooms to showcase the history of Danish royalty.

The first room to the right on the self-guided walking tour was The Rose. Formerly a ground floor dining room, The Rose was decorated in dark wood furnishings, with ornate ceiling and wall carvings of sigils and fighting deer. The room's decor had the vibe of a man's den, suiting its use in the King's Wing by the King himself.

RAFFAEL CORONELLI

The first King in question would've been King Christian IV, who ordered the construction of a Renaissance castle at the pinnacle of the era's ornate and advanced aesthetics. He also liked a good drink, lending the castle its expansive wine cellar, and even had his own signature liquor created for him. More on that last part later.

Up the stairs was a corridor that opened into a small wooden room, the Queen's Chamber, out from which one could view the ornate castle chapel. This was where Kings were anointed during its use by royalty. Its walls were covered in ceremonial coats of arms. The first King to be anointed in the chapel was Christian IV's creatively-named son Christian V.

Frederiksborg Castle chapel

HOW TO HAVE AN ADVENTURE IN SCANDINAVIA

Privy Passage and Audience Chamber from the exterior

RAFFAEL CORONELLI

Interior of the Privy Passage

HOW TO HAVE AN ADVENTURE IN SCANDINAVIA

The Audience Chamber

Leading to the Audience Chamber building was a Baroque passageway, the "Privy Passage," lined with paintings interspersed with windows looking out onto the castle's lavish gardens.

At the end of the Privy Passage was the Audience Chamber, a domed room used by the King for entertaining guests. Its bright, well-lit atmosphere drew light from large windows overlooking the garden on three sides.

Other rooms along the tour path contained multitudes of paintings and exhibits on the monarchy. One even displayed a recreation of the Runestone of Harald Bluetooth, a Viking era King who ruled from Jutland.

RAFFAEL CORONELLI

The Angel Hall

One of the more opulent rooms was designed for the Queen. Called the "Angel's Hall," this room has an ornate ceiling based on the Doge's Palace in Venice. Today, historical paintings line the wall depicting the 17th Century war between Denmark and Sweden.

An earlier war with the Swedes, the Kalmar War, is depicted in extensive tapestries in the Great Hall. The Swedes wanted these murals destroyed after the 1658 treaty of Roskilde brought peace between the two countries, presumably to get rid of what they saw as anti-Swedish propaganda, but the tapestries lived on in the castle until a fire in the 19th Century left the castle in ruins. Fully restored, I viewed their pictorial tale as I walked through the expansive hall.

HOW TO HAVE AN ADVENTURE IN SCANDINAVIA

The remainder of the rooms contained exhibits on various Danish royalty, including one on the 21st Century royal family. More interesting to me was the building itself, a flamboyant and sprawling labyrinth with aesthetic splendor covering every wall and corner.

In the downstairs gift shop, I happened upon a small bottle of King Christian IV's Mavebitter. The name means "stomach medicine," which was apparently what IV cheekily had it named to justify drinking it whenever he wanted. The actual drink is closer to an aquavit. Buying the tiny bottle and taking it home with me, I had a celebratory glass while writing this book.

I found the King's Mavebitter to have a perfume-like scent and pleasant taste, less harsh than Danish aquavits with light flavors of coriander, anise, and a floral concoction of other exotic ingredients that would've only been available to the King. These lent it a smooth drinkability. The King clearly wanted something nice and fancy to sip, and left a fine legacy of it — a liquor that tastes like the decor of the opulent renaissance palace in which it was served.

Left:
King Christian IV's Mavebitter

RAFFAEL CORONELLI

Frederiksborg Castle from the baroque garden

HOW TO HAVE AN ADVENTURE IN SCANDINAVIA

At Frederiksborg, the inside of the castle is just the beginning. Out the windows throughout, I'd caught glimpses of the vast garden that stretched behind the castle. Exiting the museum, I rounded the walls to the other side to get a closer look.

From across the lakeside moat, the castle park lay in perfect geometric organization. Baroque in design, the garden was arranged in stepped terraces up from the water.

Frederick IV was the King at Frederiksborg responsible for ordering the garden in the 1720s, commissioning it from famed royal architect Johan Cornelius Krieger.

Strong linear formations in the plants, paths, and waterfall fountain made it appear like a miniature model that could fit on a table. That all changed upon getting closer. Optical illusions in the geometric patterns caused the garden to virtually unfurl itself, a meticulous feature that the architects used to make the King's space feel larger and grander than it was.

The baroque garden at Frederiksborg

RAFFAEL CORONELLI

Right:
"Weapons Trophy",
a 19th Century recreation of
an 18th Century sculpture

Climbing the path up the outside left of the garden, I entered a maze of rectangular topiary formations at the park's highest level. The green labyrinth enveloped me, offering the occasional glimpse of the castle to give a sense of where I was. Royal stone sculptures dotted the labyrinth.

From this upper level flowed the fountain, cascading over the edges of each terrace toward the Castle Lake. I followed it down, admiring the perfect formations of each plant and rock. Gardeners buzzed about inconspicuously, performing the necessary task of keeping the garden in this exact shape and original design, all suiting the backdrop of the castle.

HOW TO HAVE AN ADVENTURE IN SCANDINAVIA

Between the majestic exterior, expansive interior, and sprawling gardens, Frederiksborg may very well be the most spectacular and opulent castle in either country I visited on the trip, if not all of Scandinavia. On a purely aesthetic level, its over-the-top Baroque sensibilities fall completely in line with the era in which it was built. Even better is that it's kept up as a museum, a place for the public to enjoy rather than something kept for housing royals who have other palaces in which to dwell.

For the first half of my day, Hillerød had shown me such splendid sights. For the afternoon, it was time to head north to Zealand's corner — to a castle with a completely different vibe, famous for completely different reasons.

To get there, I'd need to take the train north from Hillerød to Helsingør. This was a smaller train, waiting at the very edge of the station. The two-car train, almost resembling a metro line, pulled out of Hillerød Station and into the woods. The tracks cut a narrow path through the trees. Foliage closed around us.

Frederiksborg had provided magnificent aesthetic overload. The day's second and final castle would be a place with gravitas.

There are more things in heaven and Earth, Horatio, than are dreamt of in your philosophies — and some of those things are in Helsingør, Denmark.

"Helsingør" was transliterated classically by the English as "Elsinore." This spelling and the place it described was used by one William Shakespeare as the setting of his tragedy of ghosts and kings in a dark castle by the sea. Shakespeare never visited Denmark, but he did his research. The Danish prince at Helsingør served as the main protagonist of the play in his name — *Hamlet*. The building in which most of the play's action takes place was my reason for visiting the town.

The train emerged from the trees and pulled up to a shoreside station, the end of the line.

RAFFAEL CORONELLI

Kronborg Castle overlooking the Kattegat

    Exiting the station, I took one look down the street to the right and saw the specter that watched over the town, and over the sea to the east. Like the ghost of a Danish King, the walls and tower of Kronborg Castle waited.
    This was actually my second time seeing the castle; it had been the first Danish landmark I'd seen from the deck of the *Pearl Seaways*. Kronborg's positioning at the nearest point on the Kattegat between Denmark and Sweden meant that all ships from either neighboring Scandinavian country had to pass within its view.
    Across the way, I could see the Swedish shore. So, too, could Kronborg's cannon positions in the days when the two countries were not on the best of terms. A ferry to Helsingborg, Helsingør's Swedish counterpart city across the water, sat waiting to make the exceptionally short crossing. From what I could see, Swedish Helsingborg was more industrial than the Danish castle town.
    A pleasant walk by the sea drew the castle's walls closer. It was atop those walls and tower that Hamlet met the ghost of his father, contemplated mortality, delivered his soliloquy. Over the Kattegat into which he'd considered plunging, the fictional prince spoke of being or not, and what awaits in the sleep of death.
    From the moat emerged a bronze sculpture of a hand reaching up out of the water — one of the "hands of Elsinore" sculptures, installed in 2018 as a commentary on the refugee crisis.

HOW TO HAVE AN ADVENTURE IN SCANDINAVIA

Kronborg Castle

Across a moat and through an arched gate, I entered the base of the castle. A dark tunnel led through the ticketing office to the outside of the statue-lined wall of the inner courtyard. Already, the vibe was far different from bright and opulent Frederiksborg. Kronborg's atmosphere was gothic, ominous. Though Shakespeare never visited the castle himself, he'd nailed the type of story one would think to set in the place.

Shakespeare wrote *Hamlet* at the exact turn of the 17th Century, derived from the Icelandic legend of Amleth. In many ways the English writer's tribute to the Nordic world, it drew from an Old Norse poem about a Viking prince avenging his father's murder at the hands of his uncle and contemporized its elements to create a work that delved deep into the human condition.

At the time of *Hamlet*'s writing, the Renaissance Castle Kronborg at "Elsinore" was already over a hundred years old. Even before that, a 15th Century fortress occupied the strategically important spot overlooking the passage from the northern Kattegat to Copenhagen, and to the east, the Baltic Sea. This gave Denmark tabs on any ship traveling not just from Norway to Zealand, but from the Atlantic to the Baltic, from England to Russia.

RAFFAEL CORONELLI

Period carts in Kronborg's inner courtyard

The Renaissance castle was ordered to be built by King Frederick II. He needed more robust fortification and royal facilities at that important spot after the ordeal of the Northern Seven Years War between a belligerent Sweden and the united front of Denmark, Norway, Poland, and assorted Baltic states. Walls facing across the channel, the Danish could keep an eye on their eastern neighbor and all who passed. Kronborg became one of the most important castles in Europe by its sheer strategic positioning.

Through the main gate, I found myself in a spacious courtyard. Towers lined the edges, pointing into the blue sky above. A wooden cart sat as a decoration near the wall on the far side. Unlike Frederiksborg's lavish fountains, this more utilitarian castle held a subtler, atmospheric majesty.

HOW TO HAVE AN ADVENTURE IN SCANDINAVIA

Casemates entry room at Kronborg

An open door marked the entrance to the "casemates". A casemate is an artillery emplacement, these ones located in the hillside over which the castle resides. From these hidden batteries, Kronborg could fire on any passing ship. The vast subterranean passageways leading to them remain.

A brief entrance room gave a background on what lay below. Then, beckoned through an open door to a stone staircase, I descended into the dark.

Stone walls closed in. My footsteps echoed in the dimly lit blackness, illuminated only by the occasional soft orange glow of a wall-mounted lightbulb. This atmospheric lighting lead the way through the darkness. I was in Kronborg's underworld, in the shadows of the past.

Opening into a vast space, I found myself in the first sealed casemate chamber. Instead of a cannon, a looming figure occupied it, seated on a throne, bathed in spotlights.

RAFFAEL CORONELLI

Ogier the Dane, frozen in stone in the Kronborg casemates

Ogier the Dane was a mythical figure and one of several legendary Vikings whose exploits were recorded in European folklore composited from the deeds of several actual men into larger-than-life figures. In one Danish legend, he was imprisoned but later freed, as he was the last man capable of fighting a great, menacing troll.

His story reached other shores in the form of French stories, the first being *The Song of Roland* at the turn of the 11th Century. Expounded upon in later medieval French poems, Ogier was a Paladin who fought the Saracens, then wound up at Avalon where he met King Arthur. In Avalon for a time, he was a lover of Arthurian witch Morgan le Fay.

After his exploits abroad, Ogier returned to Denmark, where he was welcomed to Kronborg Castle and entered a long slumber. There, he sits, waiting to come to life again when he is most needed.

I stood in front of the ancient slumbering hero's resting place. Encased in stone, he sat in the silence of the casemates. A distant rumble permeated the chamber. Ogier did not stir, the time of his return not yet arrived. I continued on, into the cavernous dark.

HOW TO HAVE AN ADVENTURE IN SCANDINAVIA

An illuminated nook of the casemates under Kronborg Castle

The chambers wound and twisted deeper beneath Kronborg. Lamps provided a path to follow. Much of it remained encased in thick, impenetrable shadow.

RAFFAEL CORONELLI

A passageway in the Kronborg casemates

Now is the very witching time of night, when churchyards yawn and hell itself breathes out contagion to this world. (*Hamlet*, act 3, scene 2)

HOW TO HAVE AN ADVENTURE IN SCANDINAVIA

For a brief moment, I activated my phone's flashlight feature to inspect the vastness. The caverns went further back than I'd imagined, reinforced stone ceilings bored deep under the castle. I half expected the small spotlight to reveal some creature watching from the dark — or the ghost of a dead king.

Other castles can show you Crown Jewels and opulent riches. Give me one with a subterranean labyrinth where ghosts hide in unlit corners.

Around a corner from one chamber, sunlight from the outside finally filtered in. This was one of the open chambers from which artillery would've fired from a hidden point on the hillside. One of the castle's most ingenious defenses had become one of its most atmospheric attractions.

An open artillery position in the casemates

RAFFAEL CORONELLI

Interior quarters in Kronborg Castle

I returned topside, enriched by the walk through the underworld of Kronborg. Across the courtyard was the entrance to the castle's upper levels. The chambers were more relatively humble than those of opulent Frederiksborg. In these rooms, Prince Hamlet would've encountered the troubles of a turbulent life and the weight of existential dread.

The gift shop at the castle interior's exit was filled with assorted Hamlet merchandise. Everything from prop skulls, to books of the play's text, to a Hamlet manga comic book lined shelves. I'd already stocked up on souvenirs, so I did little more than window shop. It amused me to consider what Shakespeare would've thought of such a development at the time he chose the castle as his play's setting.

HOW TO HAVE AN ADVENTURE IN SCANDINAVIA

Cannons facing Helsingborg, Sweden from the Kronborg ramparts

Outside, the ramparts overlooked the ocean. Cannon positions faced out to sea, and from them, one could clearly see the industrial city Helsingborg on the shoreline of Sweden. Today, Sweden and Denmark are European Union partners and members of mutual defense treaties, which significantly changes the view's vibe from what castle occupants must've felt at the time of its construction.

Beyond the castle walls, I walked its seaside perimeter. A peninsula extended to its south. A statue of Heracles fighting the Hydra stood by the ocean, majestic pose evoking an epic battle with the monster.

I sat near the statue and viewed the castle from a short distance, a picturesque part of the Zealand coastline. This was my last time looking out at the Kattegat on the trip.

Right:
Heracles fighting the Hydra sculpture by Rudolph Tenger in Helsingør

RAFFAEL CORONELLI

Helsingør from Kronborg Castle

My day in Helsingør wasn't yet over. The castle explored, it was time to see the town.

Walking down Hestemøllestræde street from the shore, I encountered another *Hamlet*-related sight — a gorgeous mural of Sir Laurence Olivier in the title role, holding Yorick's skull, as seen in the 1948 film of the play in which he starred and directed.

Olivier's *Hamlet* is an exquisite gothic production in shadowy, expressionistic black and white. Shot like a 1940s horror film, it features what I consider to be the coolest depiction of the King's ghost in any version I've seen — a cloaked, floating skeleton puppet that emerges from a cloud of fog like a creature in a monster movie of the period. The film does not use the full text, surgically excising elements and boiling it down to a streamlined descent into human dread.

Olivier himself is magnificent, playing the role with a dark intensity, like a man burning up from inside. My favorite Hamlet, Olivier being depicted on such a grand scale in Helsingør made me like the town even more.

HOW TO HAVE AN ADVENTURE IN SCANDINAVIA

Laurence Olivier as Hamlet, mural in Helsingør

RAFFAEL CORONELLI

Bubonic Plague mural in Helsingør

Further down the street was another mural, this one of a very real horror — the Black Death. Bubonic Plague reached Denmark in 1348, and Norway one year later in 1349. Like the rest of Europe, it wrought havoc on the population and brought society to its knees. The mural depicted a plague doctor's bird mask and ailing patients.

The neighborhood around it was anything but horrific. Old medieval buildings with colorful paint jobs adorned the streets. Several cathedrals stuck up their spires, neither as scenery-dominating as the castle but still prominent landmarks.

Before long, I reached Axeltorv Square. A central town square in Helsingør, Axeltorvet was home to a statue of Erik of Pomerania, a medieval king of of both Denmark and Norway at the turn of the 15th Century. It was also home to a lovely outdoor seating area like an Italian Piazza for a food stand-like establishment.

HOW TO HAVE AN ADVENTURE IN SCANDINAVIA

Erik of Pomerania statue in Axeltorv Square, Helsingør

Hold An, as it was called, served smørrebrød. This, I decided, would be my dinner in Helsingør, and the ideal final dinner in Zealand.

Walking up to the window, a man about my age greeted me.

"Which smørrebrød would you recommend?" I asked.

"You can pick whichever ones you like," he said. "I just had the pate, which was quite nice. I also recommend the — I don't know how to say it — it's a type of meat."

That settled it. I took his two suggestions, with a third smørrebrød of smoked salmon for good measure. To drink, I had a half liter of Tuborg, a smooth Danish pilsner. Just from our brief interaction, he was one of the friendlier people I met in Denmark.

Sitting and enjoying it on the square, I drank in the medieval town around me along with my open-faced sandwiches. The man kindly brought my sandwiches out.

The pate was indeed "quite nice," a typical Danish meat mash. The cured meat smørrebrød was some type of pork, reminding me of Serrano ham. The smoked salmon was as good as any I had in Scandinavia. All were garnished with lettuce, chives, tomato, cucumber, and the works, with the pate having a large beet slice for good measure. Served over rye bread, it was a quintessential Danish meal in a quintessentially Danish place.

After dinner, I walked down Sct Olai Gade, a shopping street. I stopped into a clothing store and bought a sweater for a fairly good deal. Helsingør was a break from the bustle of Copenhagen, but big enough to have plenty to do and see. I was glad to spend my evening there before heading back to the station to catch the train to the city.

The next day, I'd be traveling to Jutland. Zealand had provided a compacted, centralized Danish experience of striking variety. None of my three days on the island had been like the others. This day of castles and legends was an indispensable installment of the trip.

On the train back, the conductor asked to see my passport, a routine check. He was a good natured man and thanked me for letting him see it.

A little while later, he announced over the intercom that a train had run over a person on the tracks at Copenhagen Central Station, delaying our train's arrival. He advised that passengers switch to the Metro to get back into the city. It was a strange note on which to end the day, though I was certainly not the one most inconvenienced by the situation.

The undiscovered country, from whose bourn no traveller returns, puzzles the will...

HOW TO HAVE AN ADVENTURE IN SCANDINAVIA

Smørrebrød from Hold An in Axeltorv Square, Helsingør

"Legende Børn" sculpture by Keld Moseholm Jørgensen in Billund, Denmark

Billund:
Back to the Beginning

I couldn't seem to catch John Hotdogs after that first taste of a classic rød on my first day in Copenhagen. John's Hotdog Deli had vanished from its spot in front of Copenhagen Central Station, the magical installation only phasing into our reality when it so pleased. I'd gotten my one taste, but I wanted to try one more Copenhagen hotdog classic before leaving — a Fransk dog.

As I stated before, I don't think French people actually eat Danish sausages stuffed into the end of buns in France, but that's what Copenhagen calls them. With John Hotdogs missing from our plane of existence, I went into Copenhagen Central Station on the morning of my leaving with luggage in hand to buy one from the only place open that served them — 7 Eleven.

7 Elevens are wildly different in various countries. The gold standard remains Japanese 7 Eleven with its Michelin star ramen (I'm not kidding). Danish 7 Eleven sold Danish sausages, though I wasn't sure what the quality would be.

Entering the train station's 7 Eleven kiosk, I ordered my Fransk dog. The clerk pulled a hotdog off a rotating grill and placed it in the signature elongated bun. Then, he asked what I wanted on it.

This may have been where things went wrong. As the foreigner in this interaction, I had no idea what a Fransk hotdog should have on it — so I imagined what a French person would put on a hotdog. This, I quickly decided, must be something along the lines of Dijon mustard.

"Gimme the spicy mustard," I motioned to the bottles on the counter.

The clerk proceeded to fill the bun with a Kattegat's worth of yellow sauce. I paid for my strange breakfast and stood outside the kiosk.

With my first bite, I found that the hotdog itself was fine. The bun was a little hard, but it was from a convenience store. Then I tasted the mustard.

Chemical spice approximating something between Grey Poupon and Tabasco seared my tastebuds. The hotdog was practically floating in it, the bun holding a Big Gulp of sauce I'd unwittingly demanded. My eyes watered. I grimaced.

So ended my tenure in Copenhagen, standing in a train station eating a bun filled with chemically hot 7 Eleven Dijon mustard soup, thinking "John Hotdogs would've done it better."

Seated in first class on the train out of the Central Station for the final time, I watched Copenhagen pull away. The conductor stopped by to check my pass — the same one I'd had the previous evening on the train back from Helsingør. He recognized me and we exchanged pleasantries.

Zealand's western side passed out the window. Darkness enveloped the train as it passed the barrier of Zealand, entering the tunnel that extends halfway between Danish islands. Light returned as we exited and emerged onto a bridge that brought us to the eastern shore of Funen.

Between Zealand and Jutland, this middle island is home to quaint small towns and agriculture. It's the birthplace of Hans Christian Andersen, giving the city of Odense a number of related tourist attractions if you choose to disembark there.

HOW TO HAVE AN ADVENTURE IN SCANDINAVIA

Canola fields on the island of Funen

Much of the land we passed around Odense was agricultural, with rolling yellow canola fields (in full bloom in May). It was a mild, pleasant view. Denmark has similar topography to Ireland or northern England. It's just a bit north in latitude and has a similar level of greenery while not being as extreme as the landscape of Norway.

The name "Odense" itself derives from Odin, as the island was one of the original Norse settlements. It was the first island visited by seafaring ancient Danes when they left the mainland. The origin of that civilization lay ahead.

There was a feeling, traveling toward Jutland, that I was going further back in time — in history, and for myself. The bridge from Odense's western shore lifted the train skyward next to Vejle Fjord, the final fjord of the trip. It was from a fjord like this one on the east coast of Jutland that the first Vikings launched their seaward expansion to the Danish islands, the Scandinavian Peninsula, and beyond.

Touching down on the shore, we'd reached the European mainland at last. Soon, we were at Vejle station. I disembarked to get the bus to my last destination — Billund.

Bus tickets could be bought at a machine in the station, but a more convenient way was to get a regional pass on the DOT app. I bought a one-day pass for the region and boarded the bus to Billund.

The bus rolled out of Vejle. The countryside wasn't remarkably different from the Danish isles, but this area connected to northern Germany held a further-reaching historical significance.

As stated at the beginning of the book, the origins of Nordic civilization came from the Germanic peoples who migrated north into Jutland. These early pre-Vikings left scant remains, but as their society evolved into the Viking Age, they left their mark in the town of Jelling in eastern Jutland.

Jelling was the seat of the first Danish Viking kings, who left runestones to their memory. These "Jelling Stones" tell of the original Viking rulers, up to and including the 10th Century stone of Harald Bluetooth.

Right: Runestone of Harald Bluetooth, reconstruction in the Museum of National History at Frederiksborg Castle

HOW TO HAVE AN ADVENTURE IN SCANDINAVIA

Passing into central Jutland, I arrived at the Billund Airport. The first order of business was to get a rapid COVID test, at that point mandatory for a flight back into the US. The testing station was hassle-free, and after a quick episode of a friendly Danish doctor cleaning out the inside of my nostrils, I was free to go in anticipation of the result in about twenty minutes. The result was negative, to my relief, but not my surprise.

It's no secret that the two countries through which I'd traveled handled the pandemic fairly well. Things were effectively back to normal by the time of my trip in spring 2022. Having to test to get back into the US after being in Norway and Denmark had a certain layer of irony. I'd end up getting my first COVID infection a couple months later at a convention in Chicago, having been completely untouched during my travels abroad.

The next order of business was a quick walk to the Zleep Hotel. This was a typical airport hotel similar to the one outside Bergen, and much better than the last place I'd stayed in Copenhagen. I dropped my bag in the luggage room and returned to the bus station bound for the town center. There was one reason in particular that had drawn me to Billund, one that would end my trip on a lighthearted note that fulfilled a certain childhood interest of mine.

One of the most recognizable staples of the 20th and 21st Centuries to emerge from Denmark was the country's invention of a new type of toy. It originated in a workshop belonging to Ole Kirk Christiansen, who began making wooden toys in Billund in 1932.

LEGO® (an abbreviation of "Leg Godt, danish for "play well") developed its novel interlocking brick system in the 1950s. It exported its line worldwide over the next couple of decades and made it a mainstay ever since.

RAFFAEL CORONELLI

The company is still headquartered in Billund, which is also the sight of the Legoland theme park. The theme park is definitely for children, but I was more interested in the museum that the company operates nearby in central Billund. That would be my destination for the afternoon, and my main activity in the town.

Boarding the bus, the driver reprimanded me for not having a signal on my phone to properly display my bus pass. A young Danish man assisted me by creating a mobile hotspot, allowing me to pull up my pass via WiFi. Sitting across from this helpful guy, we got to talking about traveling, and how he was planning a trip to visit his friends in the US. Specifically, he'd be going to the Leelanau Peninsula in Michigan, a place my family and I frequented when I was a kid. It was a nice chance interaction with a local, one that helped me get where I was going, and one that somehow tied back to an early part of my life. He alerted me to my stop, so I thanked him and disembarked.

The company headquarters isn't open to the public, but the outside of it was still worth checking out. A giant mini-figure (the stylized miniature representation of a human) towered over the entrance. Having seen the outside, I turned my attention down the street to the place where tourists are supposed to visit.

Right:
LEGO® House,
Billund

HOW TO HAVE AN ADVENTURE IN SCANDINAVIA

The author of this book outside LEGO® House in Billund

    A white building resembling a series of interconnected bricks arose from the center of the town. This innovative and appropriately themed exterior was designed by Danish architect Bjarke Ingels in the mid 2010s, with the building opening to the public in 2017. A pile of a few gigantic bricks sat by the entrance, a taste of what was in store inside.
    The interior of the entertainment complex was cavernous. At its center arose a multi-story tree made of thousands of tiny bricks, stretching across the plastic realms like Yggdrasil from Norse myth.
    After buying an admission wristband, my first stop was the basement level that houses the historical museum. Much of the museum's text was essentially PR, but it did tell the toy's history in an engaging manner. Display cases showed the original wooden toys made by hand in the Billund workshop, leading to the first plastic brick system in the 50s. Getting progressively more complex, I perused the evolution of themes I'd enjoyed as a kid in the late 90s.

A case displayed six color-coded mechanical heroes. I was exactly the right age, nine years old, when Bionicle mania hit. I distinctly remember seeing the first ad featuring Onua, Toa of Earth, clawing through a dark cave. As toyline mythos go, Bionicle's immersive lore captivated my pre-adolescent brain. I may even suggest there to be some parallel between the elemental warriors and Danish Viking myths, but I'll leave that theory half-formed in the protodermis.

Upstairs, I climbed the staircase surrounding the plastic brick world tree. Each branch held a miniature realm built on the scale of a normal set.

At the top level was a floor dedicated to one-of-a-kind creations by set designers. These took a wide variety of forms, the most prominent being gigantic Tyrannosaurus sculptures. Around the edges were artistic expressions built with the signature toy bricks — stylized scenes, interesting creatures, things that would be a little beyond a set for sale.

Back on the ground floor, a machine like one in the factory churned out a stream of red bricks. This automated demonstration gave me a free souvenir, a bag of the freshly manufactured ones to take home.

For an early dinner, the House had what might be my favorite experience in Billund — the Mini Chef restaurant.

Mini Chef is a partially automated experience; half restaurant, half robotic themed attraction. Two human-sized animatronic robots sat by a conveyer belt at the middle of the restaurant. A human waitress seated me at a table and explained the contraption next to me. A touch screen allowed me to order from their impressive beer selection, so I got a Grimbergen Double from the medieval Kronenbourg brewery in France.

The process of ordering food was different. Usually when a restaurant says "do you know how this place works?" what they mean is that they have a special soup.

HOW TO HAVE AN ADVENTURE IN SCANDINAVIA

At Mini Chef, an explanation was needed from the human waitress when she returned with my drink.

Every customer at Mini Chef gets a small bag of bricks. Each piece corresponds to a menu item. Picking one from each section, I constructed my order in a configuration that displayed the four food items I wanted — seared salmon, linguini, mushrooms, and vegetables.

I placed my construction into a tray in the computer and it whirred to life. Animations of mini figures "building" my order played on the screen while presumably real chefs cooked behind the scenes.

A little while later, the computer told me that my food would be ready. I got up and watched my bento box in the shape of a large red plastic brick descend the conveyer belt to one of robots, who pushed it to me.

This inventive means of delivery was one thing, but the food was delicious as well. I was actually shocked that what is essentially a novelty restaurant serving bento boxes via plastic robots had food as good as it was.

It wasn't lost on me what a way to end the trip this was. At the end of an adventure wherein I'd traversed arctic tundra, sailed in a Viking ship, gone to the heart of Black Metal, and faced folkloric creatures of legend, I was now a grown man sitting in a toy restaurant being served a customized bento by robots. I'd run the tonal gamut.

Almost done with my food, I ordered another beer. When the waitress brought it, it dawned on me that it might be a little strange for a grown man to sit in a toy-themed restaurant drinking beers in the late afternoon. It wasn't exactly a bar. I finished my drink and the last few nibbles of food and got up to pay the tab at the counter on the way out.

It was early evening by the time I got back to the hotel. I could've checked in and spent the rest of the night indoors, but I wanted to do one last thing on my last day in Denmark. I walked past the hotel to see what I could find.

RAFFAEL CORONELLI

Jutland, Denmark

An unmarked dirt path extended from the paved one by the hotel and into the woods, its surface so light as to barely be visible. This was it, I decided — the opportunity for one last unexpected experience in Scandinavia. I had time for one more walk though the woods.

As I meandered into the forest, I realized that my knee was just about one hundred percent better. I'd put up with it on mountains, in the arctic snow, and across cities. It had gotten to the point that I'd barely noticed it. Now, it was back to normal.

The path didn't go far. It wasn't the peak over Bergen, the mountainside of the Sognefjord, nor the reindeer fields of Kvaløya. It just went out into the woods around the hotel and came back.

Still, it was a way of saying goodbye to Scandinavia; to think about my previous hikes in the last few weeks, along with everything else. The old Norse pantheon were amongst the trees of Jutland as I bid them farvel.

Til Evighet

Early morning at Billund airport, an attendant helped me with checking my bag for my impossibly complex connecting flight through Frankfurt and Lisbon. This was a mistake, the last time I would see my bag for three weeks and all the treasures inside.

I didn't know that yet, though. Free of my larger luggage, I was content to wander the airport shop buying a couple last-minute souvenirs and, strangely, a bottle of Scottish Irn Bru — a wonderful soft drink I didn't know was available anywhere outside the UK. I guess they must get Scottish tourists at Legoland, Billund.

For breakfast, I hit up the airport terminal's Lagkagehuset coffee shop location for one last Spandauer. Sitting in view of the runway, I savored my last danish in Denmark. Knowing that made it taste all the better.

From the plane window, I took one last look at the tips of Legoland attractions sticking up from beyond the trees. Billund was an interesting place to end the trip. Such was the nature of my journey's narrative.

It was fitting, maybe, that my first trip since the pandemic delved into some darker thematic elements alongside the fun. Amidst the tribulations of the world, it's important to persevere. That was what I did on my first adventure in Scandinavia.

The plane taxied down the runway and lifted off, flying south — beyond the great, vast forest — out of Jutland, and back into Germany.

*Spirits rideth with the ones that know no fear.
They are the sons — the sons of northern darkness.*
—Immortal

HOW TO HAVE AN ADVENTURE IN SCANDINAVIA

Three weeks later...

My bag was missing. Somewhere in Frankfurt, it had missed a delayed connection and ended up in an airport storage back room. In it were souvenir gifts, shirts I'd bought at Neseblod Records and Galleri Fjalar, a bottle of Linie purchased at sea off the Norwegian coast, and a vile of King Christian IV of Denmark's Mavebitter liquor. I distinctly thought that I might never see them again, despite my constant barrage of inquiries to the airline and airports involved.

Regardless, I'd come back fuller from the experience. As with the best trips, some part of the place beyond mere souvenirs had accompanied me on my return. Spirits rideth with the ones that know no fear.

I still wanted my damned aquavit, though.

In the middle of the night, just after 12:00 AM, I received a text notifying me of a delivery. My bag had been dropped off by an O'Hare airport baggage recovery service. Dragging it inside, I tore off the tags and opened it. Nothing had been damaged, the aquavit and Mavebitter bottles perfectly intact. At last, I could enjoy the spoils of a hoard fit for a Viking.

Raffael Coronelli is a Chicago-based world adventurer and writer. His works include the *How to Have an Adventure in...* travel book series, the *Daikaiju Yuki* novel series, and essays for Anime News Network and blu-ray releases from Arrow Video.

Follow:

@RAFFLEUPAGUS

daikaijuyuki.com/raffael-coronelli

More adventures:

HOW TO HAVE AN ADVENTURE IN NORTHERN JAPAN

RAFFAEL CORONELLI

Ten cities and towns from Hokkaido to Tokyo.
Author Raffael Coronelli invites you on an adventure through Northern Japan's ancient mountain temples and frozen metropolises, journeying into local culture and cuisine — beautiful locales, pop culture touchstones, Japan-only establishments, and meeting all the people along the way.

HOW TO HAVE AN ADVENTURE IN SCOTLAND

RAFFAEL CORONELLI

AUTHOR OF *HOW TO HAVE AN ADVENTURE IN NORTHERN JAPAN*

From the Victorian city of Glasgow
to the primordial highland mists of the Isle of Skye —
Two-plus weeks in the northernmost land of the British Isles.
Whisky, rowdy Scottish parties, and bottomless lochs await.

HOW TO HAVE AN ADVENTURE IN TRANSYLVANIA

RAFFAEL CORONELLI

AUTHOR OF *HOW TO HAVE AN ADVENTURE IN SCOTLAND*

From cities at Eastern Europe's crossroads of empires to an inn at the Borgo Pass in the Carpathian Mountains — journey with author Raffael Coronelli to a land synonymous with mystery and adventure at Europe's frontier. Ensconced tradition, dark history, and famous monsters await.

COMING SOON

HOW TO HAVE AN ADVENTURE IN SCANDINAVIA 2
-SWEDEN & FINLAND-
RAFFAEL CORONELLI

Made in the USA
Monee, IL
21 September 2023